NEW DIRECTIONS FOR EVALUATION
A PUBLICATION OF THE AMERICAN EVALUATION A

D1168950

Gary T. Henry, *Georgia State University*
COEDITOR-IN-CHIEF

Jennifer C. Greene, *University of Illinois*
COEDITOR-IN-CHIEF

Outcomes of Welfare Reform for Families Who Leave TANF

George Julnes
Utah State University

E. Michael Foster
The Pennsylvania State University

EDITORS

Number 91, Fall 2001

JOSSEY-BASS
San Francisco

OUTCOMES OF WELFARE REFORM FOR FAMILIES WHO LEAVE TANF
George Julnes, E. Michael Foster (eds.)
New Directions for Evaluation, no. 91
Jennifer C. Greene, Gary T. Henry, Coeditors-in-Chief
Copyright ©2001 John Wiley & Sons, Inc.

Microfilm copies of issues and articles are available in 16mm and 35mm, as well as microfiche in 105mm, through University Microfilms Inc., 300 North Zeeb Road, Ann Arbor, Michigan 48106-1346.

New Directions for Evaluation is indexed in Contents Pages in Education, Higher Education Abstracts, and Sociological Abstracts.

Print ISSN 1097-6736; online ISSN 1534-875X at Wiley Interscience, www.interscience.wiley.com; ISBN 0-7879-5793-3

NEW DIRECTIONS FOR EVALUATION is part of The Jossey-Bass Education Series and is published quarterly by Jossey-Bass, 989 Market Street, San Francisco, California 94103-1741.

SUBSCRIPTIONS cost $69.00 for U.S./Canada/Mexico; $93 international. For institutions, agencies, and libraries, $145 U.S.; $185 Canada; $219 international. Prices subject to change.

EDITORIAL CORRESPONDENCE should be addressed to the Editors-in-Chief, Jennifer C. Greene, Department of Educational Psychology, University of Illinois, 260E Education Building, 1310 South Sixth Street, Champaign, IL 61820, or Gary T. Henry, School of Policy Studies, Georgia State University, P.O. Box 4039, Atlanta, GA 30302-4039.

www.josseybass.com

Printed in the United States of America on acid-free recycled paper containing 100 percent recovered waste paper, of which at least 20 percent is postconsumer waste.

NEW DIRECTIONS FOR EVALUATION

Sponsored by the American Evaluation Association

Editorial Policy and Procedures

New Directions for Evaluation, a quarterly sourcebook, is an official publication of the American Evaluation Association. The journal publishes empirical, methodological, and theoretical works on all aspects of evaluation. A reflective approach to evaluation is an essential strand to be woven through every volume. The editors encourage volumes that have one of three foci: (1) craft volumes that present approaches, methods, or techniques that can be applied in evaluation practice, such as the use of templates, case studies, or survey research; (2) professional issue volumes that present issues of import for the field of evaluation, such as utilization of evaluation or locus of evaluation capacity; (3) societal issue volumes that draw out the implications of intellectual, social, or cultural developments for the field of evaluation, such as the women's movement, communitarianism, or multiculturalism. A wide range of substantive domains is appropriate for *New Directions for Evaluation;* however, the domains must be of interest to a large audience within the field of evaluation. We encourage a diversity of perspectives and experiences within each volume, as well as creative bridges between evaluation and other sectors of our collective lives.

The editors do not consider or publish unsolicited single manuscripts. Each issue of the journal is devoted to a single topic, with contributions solicited, organized, reviewed, and edited by a guest editor. Issues may take any of several forms, such as a series of related chapters, a debate, or a long article followed by brief critical commentaries. In all cases, the proposals must follow a specific format, which can be obtained from the editor-in-chief. These proposals are sent to members of the editorial board and to relevant substantive experts for peer review. The process may result in acceptance, a recommendation to revise and resubmit, or rejection. However, the editors are committed to working constructively with potential guest editors to help them develop acceptable proposals.

Jennifer C. Greene, Coeditor-in-Chief
Department of Educational Psychology
University of Illinois
260E Education Building
1310 South Sixth Street
Champaign, IL 61820
e-mail:jcgreene@uiuc.edu

Gary T. Henry, Coeditor-in-Chief
School of Policy Studies
Georgia State University
P.O. Box 4039
Atlanta, GA 30302-4039
e-mail: gthenry@gsu.edu

CONTENTS

EDITORS' NOTES

This volume focuses on a series of studies of welfare reform beginning in 1998 supported by the Office of the Assistant Secretary for Program Evaluation (ASPE) of the U.S. Department of Health and Human Services. Although the details of the studies differed, they shared a common focus: the outcomes experienced by those who left cash assistance. ASPE balanced the benefits of cross-study consistency in methodology and focus with the recognition that some variation was necessary or even useful. Areas of consistency included the blending of survey and administrative data, as well as the definition of leavers of Temporary Assistance to Needy Families (TANF). The variability involved many aspects of design and measurement and provided different insights into how families fare after exiting the TANF program.

We have selected studies for this volume that highlight the strengths of the ASPE project. Although the studies are often quite consistent in their findings, the different perspectives serve to provide a richer understanding required for informed policymaking.

The first three chapters provide an overview and introduction to the volume. Chapter One presents the challenges facing evaluators of welfare reform and other large policy experiments. Primary among these is that of addressing the differing needs and expectations of stakeholders, making it particularly important to have research conducted with multiple methods and from multiple perspectives. Chapter Two, by McClintock and Lowe, elaborates this need for multiple perspectives. They argue that welfare research reflects a limited range of perspectives and suggest that additional perspectives may better address important policy questions. In Chapter Three, Isaacs provides an overview of the ASPE project.

Chapters Four and Five examine employment and recidivism. These outcomes traditionally are used as criteria for judging the success of welfare initiatives and are particularly important in economic analyses. Julnes, Fan, and Hayashi in Chapter Four and Rickman, Bross, and Foster in Chapter Five identify factors that place TANF clients at risk for recidivism and examine the relationship between recidivism and employment stability.

The next two chapters shift the focus from the stability of employment and recidivism to the well-being of former TANF clients. In recognition of the variability of outcomes, the focus also shifts from aggregate conclusions that apply to all TANF leavers to findings for subsets of TANF leavers. In Chapter Six, Rickman and Foster highlight the importance of distinguishing children as a subset of leavers, arguing that the well-being of children needs to be considered separately from the post-TANF outcomes of adults. In Chapter Seven, Julnes, Hayashi, and Anderson use cluster analysis to distinguish three groups of leavers based on self-reported well-being. Such disaggregation promotes policies that are sensitive to the needs and experiences of different groups.

The final chapters consider the policy implications of the studies that precede it. In Chapter Ten, Westra reports on efforts in Arizona to apply the findings of a leavers study in that state. Administrators in Arizona identified some of the most serious barriers to positive outcomes and developed initiatives to address those barriers. Finally, in Chapter Eleven, we summarize the findings reported in this volume and discuss the implications not only for policy but also for future research on and evaluation of welfare policies.

George Julnes
E. Michael Foster

GEORGE JULNES is assistant professor of psychology with the Research and Evaluation Methodology Program and director of the Center for Policy and Program Evaluation at Utah State University.

E. MICHAEL FOSTER is associate professor of health policy and administration at The Pennsylvania State University.

1

This chapter discusses the challenges facing evaluators of welfare reform and the ways that multiple methods can be combined to meet these challenges.

Crafting Evaluation in Support of Welfare Reform

George Julnes, E. Michael Foster

Passage and implementation of the Personal Responsibility and Work Opportunity Reconciliation Act of 1996 (PRWORA) changed the focus of welfare policy in the United States. Instead of the entitlement to cash assistance embodied in Aid to Families with Dependent Children (AFDC), Temporary Assistance to Needy Families (TANF) encourages economic self-sufficiency through employment. After five years, evidence is accumulating as to the policy's successes and failures. A key feature of this research involves the employment outcomes and well-being of welfare leavers—the mostly single women and their children who exit from welfare programs. This evidence is particularly timely; the welfare rolls have plummeted, and the law is subject to reauthorization in 2002.

Such dramatic policy changes provide evaluators with expansive opportunities for policy-relevant research, but they also raise questions about the proper role of evaluation in informing policy debates and about the types of information that are most valuable for doing so. Such questions arise in all areas of social policy, in part, because evaluations address different needs in different contexts and for different stakeholders (Mark, Henry, and Julnes, 2000). For example, in the case of welfare reform, agency administrators might value information on TANF recidivism, whereas child welfare advocates will be most concerned with measures of well-being among leavers (such as the child poverty rate). Similarly, administrators often want evaluation to serve a monitoring function that alerts them to problems in the welfare system before those problems are reported in the media. Policy specialists and academics, on the other

NEW DIRECTIONS FOR EVALUATION, no. 91, Fall 2001 © John Wiley & Sons, Inc.

hand, generally focus on the causes of poverty or why welfare initiatives help some people more than others.

These differing needs and expectations challenge evaluators. One challenge involves balancing the complexity of the research design. Policymakers may make little use of complex evaluations, while researchers may believe a simple monitoring design provides little insight into complex problems (Greenberg, Mandell, and Onstott, 2000; McClintock and Lowe, Chapter Two, this volume). Similarly, in selecting an analysis and reporting strategy, aggregate findings (for example, overall recidivism rates) have an attractive simplicity that must be balanced against the added insights of more complex analyses. For example, although policymakers are accustomed to subgroup analyses (such as distinguishing outcomes by urban versus rural regions), there are diminishing returns to adding ever finer disaggregations (reporting separate results for cross-tabulations of urban versus rural; high school diploma versus no diploma; prior work experience versus none; ages of below twenty years, between twenty and thirty years, and over thirty years old; Food Stamps receipt versus not; and ethnicity). Different stakeholders are likely to prefer different resolutions, but some balance is required (Julnes, Mark, and Henry, 1998).

Any single evaluation is unlikely to embody all methodological possibilities and research priorities. As a result, policy is best informed by an array of evaluations that use different methods. Taken separately, the different methods can be tailored for different needs; taken together, the resulting findings can be complementary and provide a fuller picture of the underlying policy and its impact. Without some coordination, however, diverse approaches can create as much confusion as insight, producing results that are difficult to reconcile or that even appear contradictory (Datta, 1997).

Recognizing the difficulties involved, this volume contributes to the welfare policy debate by reporting on a project sponsored by the Office of the Assistant Secretary for Program Evaluation (ASPE) within the U.S. Department of Health and Human Services (DHHS). This multistate project (ten states, the District of Columbia, and three large counties) involved coordinated and complementary methodologies that provide a comprehensive view of one aspect of welfare reform: the success and failure of welfare leavers. In order to address multiple needs for relevant information, the studies used multiple sources of data, employed multiple approaches to analysis, and included multiple value-based outcomes. The goals of this volume are to use this planned mixture of multiple methods to provide a richer understanding of life after TANF and illustrate how to incorporate multiple or mixed methods in the social policy arena. We introduce this volume by arguing for multiple perspectives and then describing how this volume provides an appropriate mix of perspectives in service of policy reform.

Coordinating Multiple Perspectives of Welfare Outcomes

Recent headlines have highlighted the dramatic decrease in TANF caseloads experienced nationwide ("Off Welfare, Not Faring So Well," 2000). Although these figures suggest that TANF is a success, numerous researchers have challenged this conclusion as simplistic. They argue, for example, that caseloads were declining even before PRWORA (Ellwood, 2000). They add that caseload size is a narrow indicator of program success that provides little indication of the self-sufficiency of former TANF recipients (Young, 2000).

Such debates are common in the policy arena, but it is useful to highlight one source of controversy in the current welfare debate. Much of the available information involves simple descriptive data drawn from administrative files. Although reliance in policymaking on what amounts to monitoring data has been criticized, as seen in literature on the performance measurement movement (Perrin, 1998), efforts to improve government policies increasingly rely on such data. This reliance reflects the general problem that data appropriately collected for one purpose often are employed unreflectively in service of another purpose. To improve our use of available data and guide our collection of additional data, it is important to be clear about the multiple purposes that evaluation is called on to address and the multiple methods that are available for pursuing particular sets of purposes (Mark, Henry, and Julnes, 2000). This implies a strategic approach to coordinating multiple perspectives in evaluation.

Making Use of Multiple Perspectives

The idea that evaluators are more effective when using multiple perspectives is not new. Cook and his colleagues (Cook, 1985; Shadish, Cook, and Houts, 1986) proposed *critical multiplism* as a nonfoundational approach that uses multiple perspectives to compensate for the limitations of any single perspective or method. According to Cook, this multiplism could involve value stances, program theories, operationalization of constructs, methodology paradigms, professional affiliations of investigators, and contexts for inquiry.

The basic insights of critical multiplism continue to be developed in evaluation. For example, Caracelli and Greene (1997) argue for a mixed-method approach involving the coordination of different paradigms (such as the quantitative and qualitative paradigms). Nonetheless, despite such calls for multiplism, most evaluations and policy analyses are motivated and shaped by a single tradition. In part, this narrow focus often reflects the inertia that comes from training in a particular approach to evaluation. Another obstacle is that the complexity implied by critical multiplism can be immobilizing. Without some sense of priorities, arguments for multiple methods often devolve into recommendations to "do everything." Few, if any, evaluations can or should aspire to such comprehensiveness.

Recognizing this need for guidance, evaluators have begun to develop frameworks to assist in sorting through the desired multiplisms by relating method choices to the evaluation purposes that are most appropriate in particular evaluation contexts (Mark, Henry, and Julnes, 2000). To illustrate this strategic approach to crafting multiplist evaluations, we describe the ways that multiple perspectives were coordinated in the studies reported in this volume.

Multiple Sources of Data. One critique of research on welfare leavers is that although recidivism rates are well known, little is known about the experiences of leavers in general and about those who remain off the rolls in particular (McClintock and Lowe, Chapter Two). This imbalance reflects a reliance on administrative data in studying leavers. Such data are useful in providing an overview of a limited range of outcomes, but they often provide little insight into the mechanisms responsible for the observed patterns of outcomes. As such, each of the chapters that report research (Chapters Four through Nine) uses survey data to complement administrative data. For example, in Chapter Eight, Anderson, Halter, and Schuldt use administrative data to describe the use of support services such as Food Stamps and Medicaid and survey data to understand the reasons that some eligible leavers do not use these supports.

Multiple Analyses. A second form of multiplism involves analytical methods. Given that a primary goal of these studies is to contribute to more informed policy decisions, each has some interest in providing insights into such matters as barriers to self-sufficiency or the need for outreach programs. In that the data for these studies are largely outcomes measures with some additional insights from survey questions, the evaluators face the challenge of making the most effective use of limited data. It is with regard to this goal that the studies reported here use different analyses to reveal different patterns (Julnes and Mark, 1998). For example, whereas Rickman and Foster in Chapter Six seek to strengthen their causal inferences by comparing between leavers and those who remain on TANF, Julnes, Fan, and Hayashi in Chapter Four employ structural equation modeling. Both approaches have weaknesses, and so multiplism is particularly important.

The analytical methods employed in this volume also differ in the degree of aggregation. The structural equation modeling of Julnes, Fan, and Hayashi provides a view of all leavers, whereas Rickman and Foster are concerned with a critical subgroup affected by welfare reform: the children in closed cases, particularly those children in child-only cases—that is, those in which no adult receives cash assistance. With an even greater emphasis on subgroups, Julnes, Hayashi, and Anderson in Chapter Seven employ cluster analysis to distinguish three groups of leavers: those who are satisfied and successful, those who are dissatisfied and struggling, and a large group that stands between these two extremes.

Related to disaggregation, quantitative analysts often have limited themselves unnecessarily by focusing on only one approach to revealing patterns: showing relationships between and among variables. Such methods, which include cross-tabulations, correlation coefficients, and path diagrams, are referred to as R-analyses (Rummel, 1970). However, one can also examine relationships among observations, or in this case TANF leavers, as measured across variables (Q-analysis), or even patterns over time, such as an event history analysis of recidivism of TANF leavers. Whereas most of the analyses reported here are R-analyses, the cluster analysis that Julnes, Hayashi, and Anderson use is a form of Q-analysis and so reveals different patterns: those of relationships among individuals.

Multiple Outcomes of Interest. Whereas research on welfare reform has focused on employment and recidivism, many observers have reminded us that these outcomes are not the only ones of interest. Indeed, a recent conference, described by McClintock and Lowe in Chapter Two, concluded that much more needs to be done to report on the life experiences of people who leave welfare, emphasizing the importance of the well-being of these former TANF clients, however operationalized, as an outcome of interest.

This concern with multiple outcomes of interest led us to organize this volume in these terms, beginning with two chapters that address the standard employment and recidivism outcomes and then two chapters that address leaver well-being, particularly with regard to the post-TANF well-being of certain subgroups. These chapters are then followed by two that address a third outcome of interest: use of support services that are believed important for achieving the goals of self-sufficiency and well-being. This focus on support services raises questions about bureaucratic responses that might improve access to these services. More generally, these two chapters raise the question of whether complete self-sufficiency is the proper goal of welfare reform or whether welfare reform should entail a more flexible approach that matches appropriate supports with citizens' needs.

Salutary Conclusions

In a world where evaluations have diverse purposes and evaluators must satisfy stakeholders with diverse interests, multiple perspectives are valuable and necessary. Accordingly, this volume supports this multiplism by using multiple sources of data, employing multiple approaches to analysis, and considering multiple outcomes of interest. We recognize, however, that these variations do not exhaust the range of interest. For example, all of the studies rely heavily on quantitative data (either administrative or survey) and do not include ethnography or other forms of qualitative research. Similarly, although the authors (primarily academics, but including consultants and government employees) vary in orientation, neither former nor current welfare recipients are included as authors.

Nonetheless, the chapters that follow offer a range of important findings. We begin in Chapter Two by outlining the enduring questions addressed by welfare research. In Chapter Three, Isaacs provides an overview of the broader project of which the specific studies described here are a part. We then address in Chapters Four through Nine three outcomes of interest: employment and recidivism, client well-being, and use of support services. Finally, Chapter Ten considers how such findings have been used in modifying welfare policies and Chapter Eleven explores implications of these findings for future evaluations.

References

Caracelli, V. J., and Greene, J. C. "Crafting Mixed-Method Evaluation Designs." In J. C. Greene and V. J. Caracelli (eds.), *Advances in Mixed-Method Evaluation: The Challenges and Benefits of Integrating Diverse Paradigms.* New Directions for Evaluation, no. 74. San Francisco: Jossey-Bass, 1997.

Cook, T. D. "Postpositivist Critical Multiplism." In L. Shotland and M. M. Mark (eds.), *Social Science and Social Policy.* Thousand Oaks, Calif.: Sage, 1985.

Datta, L-E. "Multimethod Evaluations: Using Case Studies Together with Other Methods." In E. Chelimsky and W. R. Shadish (eds.), *Evaluation for the Twenty-First Century: A Handbook.* Thousand Oaks, Calif.: Sage, 1997.

Ellwood, D. T. "Anti-Poverty Policy for Families in the Next Century: From Welfare to Work and Worries." *Journal of Economic Perspectives,* 2000, *14,* 187–198.

Greenberg, D., Mandell, M., and Onstott, M. "The Dissemination and Utilization of Welfare-to-Work Experiments in State Policymaking." *Journal of Policy Analysis and Management,* 2000, *19,* 367–382.

Julnes, G., and Mark, M. M. "Evaluation as Sensemaking: Knowledge Construction in a Realist World." In G. T. Henry, G. Julnes, and M. M. Mark (eds.), *Realist Evaluation: An Emerging Theory in Support of Practice.* New Directions for Evaluation, no. 78. San Francisco: Jossey-Bass, 1998.

Julnes, G., Mark, M. M., and Henry, G. T. "Promoting Realism in Evaluation: Realistic Evaluation and the Broader Context." *Evaluation,* 1998, *4,* 483–504.

Mark, M. M., Henry, G. T., and Julnes, G. *Evaluation: An Integrated Framework for Understanding, Guiding, and Improving Policies and Programs.* San Francisco: Jossey-Bass, 2000.

"Off Welfare, Not Faring So Well." *Economist,* 2000, *357,* 37.

Perrin, B. "Effective Use and Misuse of Performance Measurement." *American Journal of Evaluation,* 1998, *19,* 367–379.

Rummel, R. J. *Applied Factor Analysis.* Evanston, Ill.: Northwestern University Press, 1970.

Shadish, W. R. Jr., Cook, T. D., and Houts, A. C. "Quasi-Experimentation in a Critical Multiplist Mode." In W.M.K. Trochim (ed.), *Advances in Quasi-Experimental Design and Analysis.* New Directions for Program Evaluation, no. 31. San Francisco: Jossey-Bass, 1986.

Young, I. "New Disciplines of Work and Welfare." *Dissent,* 2000, *47,* 25–30.

GEORGE JULNES is assistant professor of psychology with the Research and Evaluation Methodology Program and director of the Center for Policy and Program Evaluation at Utah State University.

E. MICHAEL FOSTER is associate professor of health policy and administration at The Pennsylvania State University.

2

Five years after the passage of federal welfare reform, we have arrived at a vantage point that allows members of the policy-shaping community to reflect on the knowledge that evaluation research has generated, as well as the questions that remain.

Welfare Reform and Its Enduring Questions: What Have We Learned from Evaluation Research?

Charles McClintock, Staci T. Lowe

Welfare reform offers a window on the role of research-based knowledge in shaping public policy. Over the past fifteen years, program evaluation and policy analysis studies have had an intensified focus on welfare and poverty policy innovations. Experimental work flourished under the increase in waivers granted to states for experimentation with Aid to Families with Dependent Children (AFDC) policy, starting in the 1980s and culminating in the passage of the Personal Responsibility and Work Opportunity Reconciliation Act (PRWORA) in 1996. This situation created a "promised land" for evaluators, allowing them to study policy and program changes under the new Temporary Assistance for Needy Families (TANF) block grant, which were significant departures from past practice. Usually starved for large effect sizes, the work-first emphasis of TANF produced results that the typically staid world of statistical policy analysis now refers to with descriptors such as "plunging caseloads," "soaring employment," and "stunning success" (Duncan and Chase-Lansdale, 2001). Research on related changes in child support and paternity establishment shows similarly dramatic effects (Garfinkel, 2001; Zuckerman, 2000a).

With PRWORA reauthorization due in 2002, these findings provide a valuable backdrop for policymaking, serving as an antidote to speculation and ideological stubbornness on the right and the left. Yet with well over ten years of experimentation with waivers and the research on TANF, it is reasonable to ask what we have learned that is truly new. For example, we have learned that work requirements in many different forms have moved

NEW DIRECTIONS FOR EVALUATION, no. 91, Fall 2001 © John Wiley & Sons, Inc.

more people into employment than was predicted (Holzer and Stoll, 2001). Similarly, we know that employment and earnings increased dramatically for most single mothers (Haskins, 2001), but many of these same individuals have less disposable income due to cutoffs (often improper) from Food Stamps and Medicaid, as well as increases in child care and transportation costs required for work (Corcoran, Danziger, Kalil, and Seefeldt, 2000). When all is said and done, we come to the hardly surprising conclusion that requiring welfare recipients to work makes most of them work, that it costs money to make work pay, and that these gains could be reversed in a weakened economy.

To assess the extent to which our research-based knowledge is increasing or spinning its wheels, this chapter summarizes findings and issues from the domain of welfare policy in the United States by using a set of general outcome indicators and a conceptual framework drawn from the program evaluation literature.

One test of the value of applied research is the degree to which it addresses a broad range of knowledge needs and practical concerns and is useful in decision making. A previous review of research on welfare reform noted that evaluation research in the aggregate was tackling a reasonable range of knowledge utilization questions (McClintock and Colosi, 1998). The studies reviewed at that time represented questions at both policy and program implementation levels of analysis and spanned various types of research utilization such as conceptual use, instrumental use, and political use.

To continue this line of inquiry, we present a framework for appraising research knowledge from welfare reform evaluation and assessing gaps in that knowledge, both substantive and methodological. Our framework draws on the Shadish, Cook, and Leviton (1991) criteria for assessing evaluation theory and practice, and Cronbach and others' (1980) ideas about the varying interests of members within the policy-shaping community. It consists of four categories: (1) outcomes within a complex policy environment, (2) political purposes and personal values, (3) strategies and methods of evaluation research, and (4) research knowledge in agenda setting and policy implementation.

In addition to the published literature, many of our observations are referenced from a special conference held in February 2001, devoted to assessing the accumulated knowledge from research on welfare reform in preparation for the reauthorization of PRWORA.[1] In addition, we make use of preliminary findings from our study of government research requests related to welfare and poverty issues (RFPs, for short) from the U.S. Department of Health and Human Services between 1981 and 2001. These knowledge documents describe policy-related knowns and unknowns from the government's perspective and over time show enduring as well as new questions arising from policy changes such as waivers and PRWORA implementation.

Welfare Outcomes and the Policy Environment

The passage of PRWORA was one the most significant social policy developments of the twentieth century in terms of its departure from a centralized entitlement program to a system of temporary assistance that is contingent on work and based on devolution of policy to state and local governments. In addition to the welfare policy variables under study (such as work requirements), other factors important in accounting for outcomes include political history, economic growth, state and local implementation under devolution, public opinion and culture, and organizational and professional dynamics at the front line of service delivery. We summarize outcomes in the context of these factors using the Congressional Research Service categories that are linked to the policy purposes of PRWORA (U.S. Congress, 2000).

Employment and Welfare. There was broad agreement within the research and policy communities that education and training alone had not been effective policy tools for moving welfare recipients, especially parents, into the workforce (Strawn, Greenberg, and Savner, 2001). A series of waiver experiments—for example the well-publicized Greater Avenues for Independence (GAIN) program in Riverside County, California, and the National Evaluation of Welfare-to-Work Strategies (NEWWS)—suggested that job search and work strategies produced better employment outcomes than did education, at least in the short term (Riccio, Friedlander, and Freedman, 1994). These research-based findings lent support to the idea of requiring work and job searching, resulting in a work-first philosophy emphasizing the value of attachment to the labor force as an initial building block to economic independence (Pavetti, 2000). This research knowledge was consistent with a general public mood that was strongly behind requiring work as reciprocity for public assistance (Zuckerman, 2000b). Contrary to predictions in 1996 that there were not enough jobs for low-skilled welfare recipients under PRWORA work requirements, the increases in employment and decreases in welfare are now described as "unprecedented" (Blank and Schmidt, 2001, p. 72).

Given these dramatic changes, there now is a focus on how to sustain and improve employment. Current research suggests the need for a mixed strategy that links work-first activities with training in ways that lead to sustained employment (Strawn, Greenberg, and Savner, 2001). This strategy will shift responsibility for success away from broad policy mechanisms toward local implementation efforts that customize work requirements and training in ways that match recipient circumstances with employer needs and economic conditions (Holzer and Stoll, 2001).

Economic Status and Earnings. Mandating work does not necessarily improve earnings, and research is consistently supportive of the hard reality that it costs money to "make work pay" for those at the lower end of the income scale. Notwithstanding the value of income policies such as minimum wage, unemployment insurance, and earned income tax credit (EITC) or work supports such as subsidized child care and health insurance, it is safe to say that complete self-sufficiency for the working poor will remain an "elusive goal" of welfare policy (U.S. Congress, 2000, p. 1410).

The research evidence on low-income workers in general shows steady earnings increases over the 1990s, but for the lowest quintile, the results are uneven, with increases in some years and decreases in others (Haskins, 2001). With regard to overall income, child poverty rates have declined substantially and among African American children have reached the lowest levels on record, despite problems with eligible recipients getting Food Stamps and Medicaid. Effects vary considerably by state, depending on the formulas for allowing continuation of cash assistance along with earnings income, as well as the food, health, child care, and other programs that affect economic status (U.S. Congress, 2000). The bottom line appears to be that much greater gains on poverty reduction could be achieved with more attention to interpolicy coordination that focuses on low-income populations (Thompson and Gais, 2000). This idea, which is being rediscovered in the current wave of research on welfare reform, emerged as a theme in our analysis of government RFPs and also is evident in service integration arguments that have been salient for thirty years (Marquart and Konrad, 1996).

Family Formation and Structure. Passage of PRWORA was largely influenced by the increasing prevalence of nonmarital births among low-income women during the late 1980s and early 1990s and its correlation with rising welfare caseloads. Hence, two main goals in the legislation stressed a reduction in out-of-wedlock births and an increase in marriage rates. Many policy experts believed that the growth in single-parent households was in fact the primary cause of the escalation in AFDC receipt. The number of single-mother families increased from 8.4 million in 1989 to nearly 9.9 million in 1993 (U.S. Congress, 2000). Of particular concern was the apparent link between nonmarital adolescent pregnancy and long-term reliance on AFDC. In 1991, the teen birthrate (62.1 births per 1,000 women aged fifteen to nineteen) reached its highest level in two decades (Ventura, Matthews, and Curtin, 1999).

While these data seem to support the connection between increases in single parenthood and welfare receipt, subsequent to PRWORA, researchers have shown that the rise in single-parent households tells only part of the story concerning welfare growth. Specifically, the increase in AFDC caseload during the early 1990s was fueled by rapid increases in the number of child-only cases (where the parent had become ineligible) and new rules granting eligibility to two-parent families (Blank and Schmidt, 2001). This situation points to the need for more timely analysis of administrative data, especially when historical information is used in policy development.

Child Well-Being. Much of the policy debate leading up to PRWORA's implementation concerned the potential effects on children living in welfare-reliant households (Freeman, 1996; Videka-Sherman and Viggiani, 1996). Conservatives argued that a mother's employment would lead to increased family earnings, thereby preventing numerous negative child outcomes associated with poverty. Liberals feared that a mother's entry into the labor market might exacerbate the negative effects of poverty by creating additional stress in the family and reducing the time that she would be able to spend nurturing her children. While the Family Support Act (FSA) of 1988 focused attention on work requirements for mothers with young children, the studies resulting from FSA did little to inform policymakers on child-related outcomes. For example, many child outcomes from the NEWWS programs were either mixed or inconclusive (Hamilton, Freedman, and McGroder, 2000).

Similarly, a report by MDRC has generated much interest because of its finding that welfare reform does not seem to be hurting children in the ways that many child advocates and policy experts feared (Morris and others, 2001). This lack-of-harm outcome is a relatively low bar against which to measure success given the importance of promoting healthy child development, strongly suggesting that longer follow-up studies for newly working single parents are needed. Parenting and how public policy can influence it to improve children's outcomes largely remain unknown despite a considerable amount of policy research (Mayer, 1997).

Political Purposes and Personal Values

Policy interventions always embody political purposes and personal values that often engender conflict. Welfare reform, in particular, contains open conflicts around marriage, childbearing, and work, with underlying tensions about ethnicity, gender, and power. For example, there seems to be agreement from opposite ends of the ideological spectrum that nonmarital pregnancy is a serious social problem that must continue to be better understood and addressed; however, the prescriptions for designing interventions, conducting evaluative research, and ultimately refining public policy in this area differ substantially. At one extreme, Murray (2001) believes that the only way to understand more fully the relationship between welfare receipt and family formation issues, such as nonmarital pregnancy, is to implement a radical social experiment in which some states cut off all benefits for unmarried mothers.

Mead (2001) asserts that the reform elements that resonate most clearly with the public (such as government support for the poor in exchange for work from adults) are also the most likely to experience success. One could argue that the more contentious or value laden the issue is, the less likely it is that research-based knowledge is to be used. Some components of PRWORA, such as the work-first provision, were backed by empirical data from pre-TANF welfare reform experiments. In contrast, the bulk of pre-TANF research on family formation and structure did not demonstrate changes in the formation of two-parent families (U.S. Congress, 2000). For example, evaluations of abstinence-only pregnancy-prevention programs and family cap policies yielded inconclusive results (Kirby, 1997; U.S. Congress, 2000).

Evaluation Strategies and Methods

At the New World of Welfare Conference for policy analysts and scholars held in February 2001, welfare recipients and advocacy groups showed up and demanded a voice. Conference organizers provided registration and speaking time for these participants. Unfortunately, it was clear that the academic-policy culture and the welfare advocacy–service culture had different methods of discourse. Our observations of these conference events illustrate several of the challenges for evaluation strategies and methods.

Both groups agreed that post-PRWORA, there are many current and former recipients who are worse off (or at least no better), that some abuses have occurred in relation to diversion from welfare and denial of other benefits, and that PRWORA reauthorization needs to address critical work supports such as accessible child care and improved procedures for obtaining Food Stamps and Medicaid (or low-income federal and state health insurance programs).

The voices of the protestors were in part aimed at a missing evaluation strategy. There were no qualitative or ethnographic studies in which the lives of welfare recipients were depicted more fully in both their hardships and their strengths. Welfare recipients took strong exception to the use of extreme adjectives such as "stunning success" in caseload decline without more detailed discussion of those who might have been denied benefits illegally or accounts of struggles among those worse off under TANF. To say, as some research did, that 60 percent of welfare leavers are better off (and those data are typically disputed in various ways) means that 40 percent are not, and relatively little information was presented about that large number of individuals who likely face considerable economic and social stress. There was little mention of mixed-methods strategies in which statistical modeling results were brought to life with interview and observation data about these groups. Moreover, many of the analyses do not include churners (recipients who return to the rolls within a month), which results in an underexamination of those who are potentially most in need and constitute at least part of the hardest-to-serve population.

The importance of administrative data for program evaluation has been recognized for at least the past two decades. For example, we found several federal RFPs from the early 1980s detailing the need for better tools and systems of record keeping as a means of preventing welfare fraud. More recently, there has been an increased emphasis on sophisticated information technology systems for the improved operation of child support enforcement, as well as for tracking leavers and churners. Survey data from a variety of national sources, including the Current Population Survey and Panel Study of Income Dynamics, continue to be widely used in welfare research (Winn and Lennon, 2000). Combinations of survey and administrative data are becoming more common, although technical challenges make it difficult to define common units of analysis, time periods, and geographical boundaries (Moffit and Ver Ploeg, 1999; U.S. General Accounting Office, 2000).

A prime example of where more could be done is child care, an area that everyone agrees is crucial to maintaining steady work but is bereft of good national and state data on availability, use, cost, and outcomes on employment and child well-being (Besharov and Samari, 2001).

A promising sign of future methodological heterogeneity shows up in our analysis of government RFPs. During the past five years, there appears to be interest in the full range of methodological strategies described in this chapter, in addition to continuing rigorous experimental work where meaningful comparison group conditions can be created. This finding suggests that policymakers take seriously the critical multiplism and mixed-methods strategies that have been developed in the field of program evaluation (Cook, 1985).

Research Knowledge in Agenda Setting and Policy Implementation

Research-based knowledge has had an important influence on welfare agenda setting, including PRWORA's predecessor, the 1988 Family Support Act (Haskins, 1991), but it also faces significant limits in relation to the policy environment and implementation processes. This is especially true with respect to research on broad social problems—such as poverty—that are influenced by a complex and interactive multipolicy environment as well as by economic and cultural change (Albert, 2000).

Research findings are most likely to influence policy agenda setting when political and policy coalitions are aligned to support change in the intergovernmental system that maintains this status quo (Sabatier, 1988). For instance, in a study of how state policymakers used evaluations of welfare reform experiments such as California's GAIN program (Greenberg, Mandell, and Onstott, 2000), there was more interest in the political and bureaucratic feasibility of the program than in its outcomes (assuming, at least, that they did no harm). In this sense, policy research becomes more like historical or cultural inquiry and, in spite of its sophisticated design, measurement, and analysis tools, appears to serve primarily as a sensitizing device for practitioners who use their tacit knowledge of policy implementation to address the challenges of politics, cross-policy coordination, and organizational and front-line service delivery dynamics (McClintock, 2000).

Notwithstanding this limitation, there are several important themes evident in our analysis of the research literature and federal government RFPs on welfare, including issues that appear to be more or less settled as well as long-standing questions and possible limits of research knowledge given the complex environment of family and social welfare. Each of the following examples illustrates both what we have learned and what has remained resistant to understanding or influence from research.

• Public policy designed to assist low-income individuals and families is a changing patchwork environment that makes it difficult to evaluate the impact of any single policy. For instance, in addition to reauthorization of PRWORA, the child care block grant and Food Stamp programs are due for legislative review. These programs are crucial to the impact of PRWORA on poverty and other outcomes, as are many other policies such as child support collection, adoption, Medicaid and low-income health insurance, income disregards, EITC, minimum wage, unemployment insurance, housing and energy assistance, and other educational, child welfare, family, and social programs. This system of multiple legislative authorization and regulation makes it very difficult for states and localities to coordinate services, as well as to conduct collaborative case management across public and private sectors for the most needy. Given this complex policy environment, it is difficult to evaluate the effects of a single policy (such as TANF) or policy element (such as work requirements), at least insofar as the results would be different given changes in the many other policies that impinge on outcomes of interest.

• The dramatic changes in employment related to welfare reform were strongly influenced by a robust economy in the latter half of the 1990s and by cultural and bureaucratic changes that led many potentially eligible recipients to divert themselves from applying for public assistance. Despite the volume of research documenting these changes, many uncertainties remain, such as the following:

What is happening to leavers and diverters who have not found employment?

What will happen to employment gains in an economic downturn, and how will TANF policies such as time limits and sanctions need to be modified?

What is the long-term impact of employment requirements on income and child outcomes for the lowest-paid-income single mothers, especially those with very young children?

What organizational, managerial, and service delivery capacities are needed at state and local levels of government to maintain the employment goals of PRWORA while retaining an effective safety net for those left behind?

What are effective systems for national, state, and community data collection that will allow tracking and program evaluation, and how should such systems connect survey, ethnographic, and administrative data for a more complete analysis of welfare and poverty outcomes?

• Public assistance recipients with multiple problems such as substance abuse, mental illness, and low cognitive functioning are unlikely ever to maintain stable employment. It seems likely that poverty policy in the United States is moving toward a two-tiered system with emphasis and support for work for those deemed in need of temporary assistance and another system that expands Supplemental Security Income (SSI), perhaps including sheltered work, for those whose needs are less tractable.

• Outreach in relation to parenting and family functioning that prevents dependency on welfare and improves child outcomes remains a major policy challenge, despite evidence of long-term cost-effectiveness for some forms of intervention (Olds and others, 1997). Research to date suggests that PRWORA has done no harm (for example, child abuse and neglect rates have not increased), but it is not clear yet that the policy changes have improved well-being (for example, child development outcomes have not consistently improved). Some recent findings have challenged assumptions about the impact of case management and support for parenting on child outcomes that researchers and practitioners would have taken as settled knowledge (St. Pierre, Layzer, Goodson, and Bernstein, 1999).

Hence, despite some consistent support, research knowledge seems to have provided only tenuous understanding of the complex dynamics within families and between families and community services, especially as they might improve parenting. Indeed, it is possible that social policy has a very limited role in influencing parenting, family formation, and child outcomes, in contrast with cultural and economic influences such as the increase of women in the paid workforce, norms about marriage and onset of sexual activity, and reductions in employment opportunities for lower-skilled individuals. Research knowledge has confirmed that these are complex multivariate issues but has provided little specific guidance on action.

Conclusion

This review of research on welfare illustrates that we have gained new knowledge about the effects of requiring work that complements a previously established understanding that guaranteed public assistance is a disincentive to work. At the same time, research findings appear mainly to be resensitizing us to enduring questions that have been raised for many years but are politically unresolved in the policy-shaping community. With all eyes focused on the reauthorization of PRWORA in 2002, we recommend a policy and research agenda that emphasizes five recurring issues:

1. The interactive effects on poverty among a variety of social welfare policies, intergovernmental relations, and economic conditions
2. The fact that it costs money to make work pay for those who are able
3. The need for a new approach for those with enduring multiple barriers to self-sufficiency

4. The challenge of doing more than "no harm" for poor children and improving parenting and child outcomes
5. A more multiplistic empirical picture of various subsets of the welfare population based on improved linkage of administrative and survey data, ethnographic and other forms of qualitative inquiry, and analysis of community context

We trust that the conceptual framework used to arrive at these conclusions can improve both the policy and research agendas. For many of these issues, additional research is less important than the political will to continue bold policy innovation that grapples with previous findings about how to support and make work pay for those who are able and how to care for those who are not.

Note

1. The New World of Welfare Conference: An Agenda for Reauthorization and Beyond, organized by the Ford School of Public Policy at the University of Michigan, Annie E. Casey Foundation, and the Charles Stewart Mott Foundation.

References

Albert, V. N. "The Role of the Economy and Welfare Policies in Shaping Welfare Caseloads: The California Experience." *Social Work Research,* 2000, *24,* 197–210.

Besharov, D., and Samari, N. "Welfare Reform and Child Well-Being." Paper presented at the New World of Welfare Conference, Washington, D.C., Feb. 2000.

Blank, R., and Schmidt, L. "Work, Wages and Welfare Reform." Paper presented at the New World of Welfare Conference, Washington, D.C., Feb. 2000.

Cook, T. D. "Postpositivist Critical Multiplism." In L. Shotland and M. M. Mark (eds.), *Social Science and Social Policy.* Thousand Oaks, Calif.: Sage, 1985.

Corcoran, M., Danziger, S. K., Kalil, A., and Seefeldt, K. S. "How Welfare Reform Is Affecting Women's Work." *Annual Review of Sociology,* 2000, *26,* 241–269.

Cronbach, L. J., and others. *Toward Reform of Program Evaluation.* San Francisco: Jossey-Bass, 1980.

Duncan, G. J., and Chase-Lansdale, P. L. "Welfare Reform and Child Well-Being." Paper presented at the New World of Welfare Conference, Washington, D.C., Feb. 2000.

Family Support Act of 1988, P.L. No. 100–485. 102 Stat. 2343. 1988.

Freeman, E. M. "Welfare Reform and Services for Children and families: Setting a New Practice, Research, and Policy Agenda." *Social Work,* 1996, *4,* 521–532.

Garfinkel, I. "Assuring Child Support in the New World of Welfare." Paper presented at the New World of Welfare Conference, Washington, D.C., Feb. 2001.

Greenberg, D., Mandell, M., and Onstott, M. "The Dissemination and Utilization of Welfare-to-Work Experiments in State Policymaking." *Journal of Policy Analysis and Management,* 2000, *19,* 367–382.

Hamilton, G., Freedman, S., and McGroder, S. M. *Do Mandatory Welfare-to-Work Programs Affect the Well-Being of Children? A Synthesis of Child Research Conducted as Part of the National Evaluation of Welfare-to-Work Strategies.* New York: Manpower Demonstration Research Corporation, 2000.

Haskins, R. "Congress Writes a Law: Research and Welfare Reform." *Journal of Policy Analysis and Management,* 1991, *10,* 616–632.

Haskins, R. "The Second Most Important Issue: Effects of Welfare Reform on Family Income and Poverty." Paper presented at the New World of Welfare Conference, Washington, D.C., Feb. 2001.

Holzer, H. J., and Stoll, M. A. (*Employers and Welfare Recipients: The Effects of Welfare Reform in the Workplace.* San Francisco: Public Policy Institute of California, 2001.

Kirby, D. *No Easy Answers: Research Findings on Programs to Reduce Teen Pregnancy.* Washington, D.C.: National Campaign to Prevent Teen Pregnancy, 1997.

Marquart J. M., and Konrad E. L. (eds.). *Evaluating Initiatives to Integrate Human Services.* New Directions for Program Evaluation, no. 69. San Francisco: Jossey-Bass, 1996.

Mayer, S . E. *What Money Can't Buy: Family Income and Children's Life Chances.* Cambridge, Mass.: Harvard University Press, 1997.

McClintock, C. *Research and Practitioner Knowledge About Collaboration: Educating Professionals for Policy Management and Implementation.* Seattle, Wash.: Conference of the Association for Public Policy Analysis and Management, Nov. 2000.

McClintock, C., and Colosi, L. A. "Evaluation of Welfare Reform: A Framework for Addressing the Urgent and the Important." *Evaluation Review,* 1998, 22, 668–694.

Mead, L. M. "The Politics of Conservative Welfare Reform." Paper presented at the New World of Welfare Conference, Washington, D.C., Feb. 2001.

Moffit, R. A., and Ver Ploeg, M. (eds.). *Evaluating Welfare Reform: A Framework and Review of Current Work.* Washington, D.C.: National Academy Press, 1999.

Morris, P. A., and others. *How Welfare and Work Policies Affect Children: A Synthesis of Research.* New York: Manpower Demonstration Research Corporation, 2001.

Murray, C. "Family Formation Issues and Welfare Reform." Paper presented at the New World of Welfare Conference, Washington, D.C., Feb. 2001.

Olds, D. L., and others. "Long-Term Effects of Home Visitation on Maternal Life Course and Child Abuse and Neglect." *Journal of the American Medical Association,* 1997, 278, 637–643.

Pavetti, L. A. "Creating a New Welfare Reality: Early Implementation of the Temporary Assistance for Needy Families program." *Journal of Social Issues,* 2000, 56, 601–615.

Personal Responsibility and Work Opportunity Reconciliation Act of 1996, Pub. L. No. 104–193, 110 Stat. 328 (1996).

Riccio, J., Friedlander, D., and Freedman, S. *GAIN: Benefits, Costs and Three-Year Impacts of a Welfare-to-Work Program.* New York: Manpower Demonstration Research Corporation, 1994.

Sabatier, P. A. "An Advocacy Coalition Framework of Policy Change and the Role of Policy-Oriented Learning Therein." *Policy Sciences,* 1988, 21, 129–168.

Shadish, W. R., Cook, T. D., and Leviton, L. C. *Foundations of Program Evaluation: Theories of Practice.* Thousand Oaks, Calif.: Sage, 1991.

St. Pierre, R. G., Layzer, J. I., Goodson, B. D., and Bernstein, L. S. "The Effectiveness of Comprehensive, Case Management Interventions: Evidence from the National Evaluation of the Comprehensive Child Development Program." *American Journal of Evaluation,* 1991, 20, 15–34.

Strawn J., Greenberg, M., and Savner, S. "Improving Employment Outcomes Under TANF." Paper presented at the New World of Welfare Conference, Washington, D.C., Feb. 2001.

Thompson, F. J., and Gais, T. L. "Federalism and the Safety Net: Delinkage and Participation Rates." *Publius—The Journal of Federalism,* 2000, 3, 119–142.

U.S. Congress. House of Representatives. Committee on Ways and Means. *2000 Green Book.* Washington, D.C.: U.S. Government Printing Office, 2000.

U.S. General Accounting Office. *Welfare Reform: Improving State Automated Systems Requires Coordinated Federal Effort.* Washington, D.C.: U.S. General Accounting Office, 2000.

Ventura, S. J., Matthews, T. J., and Curtin, S. C. "Declines in Teenage Birth Rates, 1991–98: Update of National and State Trends." *National Vital Statistics Reports,* 47 (26). Hyattsville, Md.: National Center for Health Statistics, 1999.

Videka-Sherman, L., and Viggiani, P. "The Impact of Federal Policy Changes on Children: Research Needs for the Future." *Social Work*, 1996, *41*, 594–600.

Winn, E., and Lennon, M. C. "The Role of Administrative Data and National Data Sets in Understanding Welfare Reform." *Forum* (Research Forum on Children, Families, and the New Federalism), 2000, *3*.

Zuckerman, D. M. "The Evolution of Welfare Reform: Policy Changes and Current Knowledge." *Journal of Social Issues*, 2000a, *56*, 811–820.

Zuckerman, D. M. (2000b). "Welfare Reform in America: A Clash of Politics and Research." *Journal of Social Issues*, 2000b, *56*, 587–599.

CHARLES MCCLINTOCK is dean of the School of Human and Organization Development at Fielding Graduate Institute and professor emeritus in the Department of Policy Analysis and Management at Cornell University.

STACI T. LOWE is a doctoral student in policy analysis and management at Cornell University, with interests in social policy and program evaluation.

3

Fourteen states and large counties received federal funding in 1998 to use a combination of administrative and survey data to monitor the condition of families leaving welfare. This chapter provides an overview of these studies.

Cross-State Findings on Families Leaving Welfare

Julia B. Isaacs

As large numbers of recipients leave the welfare rolls, interest in their circumstances is widespread. Are individuals working? Are they and their families moving out of poverty? How are their children faring? Do they continue to need and receive assistance through other programs? To answer these questions, the Office of the Assistant Secretary for Planning and Evaluation (ASPE), Department of Health and Human Services (HHS), awarded $2.9 million in grants in fiscal year 1998 to fourteen states and large counties to track and monitor outcomes among families leaving welfare.[1] Funded out of a special congressional appropriation, these grants were designed to collect data documenting what was happening to poor families after the sweeping changes in welfare legislation.

This chapter provides an overview of the design of the ASPE-funded leavers studies and reviews major cross-study findings in three areas: employment, program participation, and household income. In each area, the chapter discusses how data from administrative records are enriched by the more detailed findings emerging from surveys of former recipients.

Overview of Research Strategy

Following the devolution of welfare programs to the state level, ASPE chose a research strategy that combined local flexibility in study design with some national direction and coordination. All fourteen projects used administrative

---

The views expressed in this chapter are those of the author and should not be construed as representing the views of the Department of Health and Human Services or any office therein.

data to track an early cohort of individuals who left welfare around 1996 or 1997 and combined administrative and survey data to track the economic status and general well-being of at least one cohort leaving welfare one to two years later. Projects varied, however, in the number and types of administrative data sets examined and the design of the surveys of former recipients.[2] All researchers collected data across multiple dimensions, including employment, program participation, economic status, family structure, child well-being, material hardship, and barriers to employment. However, projects designed their own survey instruments, which differed in wording and emphasis. Although this diversity poses challenges for summarizing results nationally, it has allowed states to meet the demands of their own governors and legislators for timely information on families leaving their state's welfare program.

Although each study had its own methodology, federal staff took certain steps to promote cross-project comparability. Chief among these was developing consensus around a common definition of the leaver study population as "all cases that leave cash assistance for at least two months." This definition excludes cases that reopen within one or two months; such cases are more likely closed due to administrative churning than to true exits from welfare. In addition, through national meetings and an electronic listserv, ASPE staff facilitated peer networking among researchers, promoted the use of nationally developed questions on topics such as food security and child well-being, and encouraged standardized reporting of certain administrative data outcomes.

Federal guidance was developed in collaboration with grantees and offered as suggestions rather than mandates. In fact, state researchers were more receptive to cross-project coordination and national direction than originally expected. Still, the particular nature of their project design or nuances of their state's policies or administrative data prevented most grantees from fully adopting ASPE's recommendations.

Any attempt to examine outcome across states therefore must recognize that observed cross-site differences may reflect methodological differences. Outcomes also may be affected by a region's economy or the characteristics of its caseload. The experience of leaving welfare may differ between urban and rural areas or between English- and non-English-speaking recipients.

Finally, cross-state differences in outcomes may reflect policy differences. For example, a state's sanctioning policy may affect the leaver population, especially in states that remove noncompliant families from the rolls.

Although linking between-state differences in outcomes to policy differences can be tempting, this linkage is not the primary purpose of the ASPE-funded studies. Projects observed outcomes across the entire population of leavers, all of whom were affected by the widely publicized changes to end welfare as we know it. No study conducted a controlled experiment comparing former recipients who participated in experimental program X with a randomly assigned group who participated in control program Y. Although one can compare early and late cohorts of leavers, it is difficult to know whether observed differences in outcomes reflect changes in policies, economic conditions, or caseload composition. As shown in other chapters, statistical analyses allow examination of regional or subgroup differences within a state. Such multivariate analyses have not been conducted across the states, however.

In essence, the studies were designed to serve a monitoring function, describing outcomes for families affected by welfare reform, rather than an evaluative one, describing the impacts of reform. This monitoring function was critical in the light of uncertainty about how poor children and their families would fare after the federal entitlement to welfare was ended. Through the leavers studies, information was collected across multiple dimensions of economic and family well-being for an important segment of the low-income population.[3] Cross-site findings for three dimensions—employment, program participation, and income—are discussed in the remainder of this chapter.

Employment

Employment outcomes have been quite consistent across the fourteen studies. According to administrative data (see Table 3.1), employment rates of former recipients ranged from 46 to 68 percent. Moreover, employment rates remained fairly constant across the first four quarters after exit in all study areas. This finding does not mean that the same 50 to 60 percent of leavers were employed every quarter. Some former recipients lost their jobs, while others found new employment, with the result that 62 to 90 percent of leavers had earnings in at least one of the first four quarters after exit. Between 31 and 47 percent of leavers were employed in all four quarters, according to the eight studies reporting this statistic (data not shown).

Three of six jurisdictions analyzing employment across multiple cohorts found that recipients leaving welfare in 1998 had higher employment rates—by 5 to 10 percentage points—than those leaving in 1996. Two other jurisdictions, however, found no change, and one found a decrease in employment.

Administrative data capture only earnings reported to the state unemployment insurance systems and therefore do not capture earnings from certain professions (for example, self-employment, federal employment, agricultural work, or domestic service) or work across state lines. In fact, between 57 and 71 percent of former recipients reported working at time of interview. In all but one study (see Table 3.1), these rates were higher than those observed in administrative data. The vast majority of leavers—85 to 92 percent—reported being employed at least once since exit. In addition, three studies found that the household employment rate (counting the earnings of anyone in the household) was 9 to 15 percentage points higher than that for the leaver herself or about 72 to 80 percent (data not shown).

Table 3.1. Employment Rates of Leavers

Grantee and Cohort[a]	Administrative Data					Survey Data	
	First Quarter Post exit	Second Quarter Post exit	Third Quarter Post exit	Fourth Quarter Post exit	Any of Four Quarters	Employed at Interview	Employed Since Exit
Arizona, 96.4	58.2	55.8	55.1	55.4	74.7		
Arizona, 98.1	53.1	51.0	51.7	50.1	73.3	58.0	
Florida, 97.2	50.2	50.8	52.8	53.6	70.5	56.7	
Georgia, 97.1	63.0	59.0	58.0	57.0	75.0		
Georgia, 99.1–00.1	61.0	63.0	59.0	59.0		69.0	
Illinois, 97.3–98.4	53.6	52.9	53.0	54.1	69.1	63.0	85.0
Massachusetts, 99.1	59.9	60.6	51.2		67.8	71.0	
Missouri, 96.4	58.1	57.7	58.6	57.8	73.4	65.0	90.0
New York, 97.1	50.0	49.0	48.0	48.0	62.0		
South Carolina, 98.4–99.1	66.7	67.6	66.9	63.2	90.0	60.0	
Washington State, 96.4	52.0	52.0	55.0	56.0	68.2		
Washington State, 98.4	62.0	58.0				59.0	86.0
Wisconsin, 95.3–96.2	63.2	61.5	61.3	61.6	75.3		
Cuyahoga, 96.3	59.3	54.2	55.8	56.8	71.7		
Cuyahoga, 98.3	68.3	64.1	66.8	64.2	81.7	70.0	92.0
Washington, D.C., 97.4	54.4	57.8	50.0	52.3		60.3	
Los Angeles, 96.4	47.2	45.5	46.3	46.6			
San Mateo County, 96.4	49.6	49.9	48.4	50.3	67.1		
San Mateo 98.4	54.6	54.7	54.6			56.9	

Note: Rates are for single-parent leavers, except that Illinois, Massachusetts, Missouri, and Washington, D.C., include small percentages of two-parent leavers. Those with any earnings in state unemployment insurance systems are considered employed except that Cuyahoga County and Los Angeles County require more than $100 per quarter, Washington State also counts earnings reported to the welfare system, and Washington, D.C., uses data from the *National Directory of New Hires.* Washington, D.C., employment rates would be 8 percentage points higher if leavers without social security numbers were excluded from the denominator, as they are in New York, Missouri, and possibly other studies.

[a]The numbers following the grantee name refer to dates. For example, "96.4" means cases existing in the fourth quarter of 1996.

Among former recipients with jobs, median quarterly earnings in the first quarter after exit ranged from $1,900 in South Carolina to $3,400 in Washington, D.C. Quarterly earnings rose during the year following exit in all locations. Median hourly wages, as reported in survey data from eight studies, ranged from $6.50 to $9.00 an hour. Former recipients with jobs worked an average of thirty-three to thirty-nine hours per week; median hours averaged forty hours per week.[4]

In sum, the studies consistently found that about three-fifths of leavers were working, and generally forty hours per week, but at relatively low wages and with intermittent joblessness. To what extent do families with these patterns of employment and earnings support themselves, and to what extent do they rely on government programs for support?

Program Participation

According to data from thirteen jurisdictions, between 3 and 20 percent of families leaving welfare returned to cash assistance within one quarter. Rates of welfare receipt rose to between 9 and 28 percent in the next quarter. Rates rose very slightly over the next six months, reaching 11 to 29 percent one year after exit. Because some people return to the rolls and then leave again, the proportion that ever returned within the first year after exit was higher, ranging from 17 to 38 percent.

Comparisons of early and late cohorts reveal no clear pattern of returns to welfare. As compared with earlier cohorts, recidivism among 1998 leavers was higher in three states but lower in three others. (No trend was apparent in two others.)

Although the majority of leavers remained off cash assistance, most received other government support. One of the most common was Medicaid, although rates of participation varied considerably across states. As shown in Table 3.2, between 41 and 76 percent of adult leavers were enrolled in Medicaid in their first quarter post exit. In most areas, adult enrollment rates dropped 10 percentage points or more by the fourth quarter after exit. Medicaid coverage varied even more dramatically in survey data, ranging from 33 percent in Missouri (measured over two years after exit) to 81 percent in Massachusetts (measured slightly under a year after exit). A higher percentage of surveyed leavers—51 to 85 percent—reported Medicaid coverage for their children.

Lack of Medicaid enrollment might not be a problem if leavers had health insurance through employment or other means. However, only 20 to 34 percent of leavers reported employer-sponsored or other insurance; slightly fewer (7 to 28 percent) reported such coverage for their children. These figures reveal that large numbers of former recipients and their children were without health insurance. The percentage of adult leavers without insurance ranged from 7 to 45 percent; rates for children ranged from 8 to 33 percent. The lack of health insurance was more prevalent in states with low Medicaid enrollment rates (see Table 3.2).

The variation in Medicaid enrollment can be explained somewhat by differences in survey methodology (for example, timing and wording of survey) or in the linking and analysis of administrative data.[5] Still, the observed cross-state variation is too wide to be solely attributable to methodological differences. Some variation likely reflects differences in Medicaid eligibility

Table 3.2. Adult and Child Health Insurance Status

	Administrative Data		Survey Data			
Grantee and Cohort*	Medicaid 1st Qtr post exit	Medicaid 4th Qtr post exit	Medicaid at Inter-view	Employer Sponsored Insurance	Other Insurance	No Insurance
Arizona 96.4	58	47				
Arizona 98.1 **	54	40	39(51)	15(12)	5(8)	40(26)
Ill.97.3–98.4	58	40	47(53)	***	21(23)	36(29)
Georg.99.1–00.1			66(82)	(4)	(3)	24(11)
Florida 97.2	55	46	(57)			45(33)
Mass. 99.1			81(83)			7(8)
Missouri 96.4	42(85)	39(86)	33(68)	25(14)	9(9)	32(11)
New York 97.1		35(34)				
S.Car.98.4–99.1	69(88)	45(68)	(85)			
Washington 97.4	53	40				
Washington 98.4	60		56(67)	13(9)	8(11)	26(13)
Wisc. 95.3–96.2	76	63				
Cuyahoga 96.3	41	42				
Cuyahoga 98.3	60	46				
D.C. 97.4	(35)	(38)				
D.C. 98.4	(42)	(48)	54(60)	19(12)	4(11)	22(16)
San Mateo 98.4	(76)	(59)	(64)	***	(28)	(9)

Notes: Insurance status for children, shown in ( ), are percentages of adult leavers with at least one child in Medicaid (or one member of family, in DC and San Mateo). SCHIP is counted as Medicaid in most surveys. Rates are for single-parent leavers, except that Illinois, Massachusetts, Missouri, Washington, and D.C. include small percentages of two-parent leavers.

* Cohort "96.4" means cases existing fourth quarter of 1996.

** Arizona data include leavers who return to TANF after one month, as well as the traditional two-month leave.

*** Rates for employer-sponsored insurance included in "other."

(which is set by states) and in administrative practices, which vary across states and local areas.

Findings from the leavers studies and other research have prompted federal and state initiatives to ensure that families leaving welfare are not incorrectly denied Medicaid benefits. In their leavers' reports, several states mention changes in policies or procedures designed to increase Medicaid enrollment among future leaver cohorts. Comparisons of 1996 and 1998 cohorts show increased Medicaid enrollment in three jurisdictions, no change in one, and decreased enrollment in another.

Participation in other forms of government assistance was also common but generally at lower levels than for Medicaid. For example, in most studies, between one-third and slightly over one-half of leavers received Food Stamps immediately after exit. Similar rates were found in both administrative and survey data. As with Medicaid, receipt of Food Stamps declined over the year following exit, particularly among those remaining off cash assistance. According to several surveys, other common forms of assistance included free- and reduced-price lunches (43 to 87 percent of leavers), the federal earned income tax credit (EITC; 32 to 65 percent), housing assistance (16 to 60 percent), and Supplemental Security Income (SSI; 2 to 12 percent). In addition, between 11 and 35 percent of former recipients reported receiving child support, often secured with help from the child support enforcement agency. Income from these sources can be an important component of household income.

Household Income

Total household income is difficult to measure, particularly in leaver households. Paychecks can vary from month to month, and variations in unearned income and household composition may generate added instability. Nevertheless, ASPE encouraged researchers to collect survey data on this critical measure of family well-being.

As shown in Table 3.3, average household cash income of former recipients ranged from $964 to $1,427 per month across seven studies. Median household incomes were about $200 lower. Although Food Stamp benefits are not included as cash income, they provided the average household with an additional $100 to $129 per month according to two studies.

Five of the seven studies asked detailed questions probing for income from various sources, and two simply asked for total household income. Consistent with past research, the surveys that asked multiple questions uncovered higher levels of income. This variation suggests that the lower incomes found in Illinois and Washington, D.C., may reflect differences in income reporting rather than true differences in income.

Three of the studies with comprehensive income questions also calculated the percentage of households with income below the poverty line. Although researchers measured poverty in slightly different ways, all three reported a poverty rate of 57 or 58 percent. (The Cuyahoga measure was based on cash income plus Food Stamps, while the Washington State and Missouri rates were based on cash income only.)

Although these poverty rates are quite high, one study (Washington State) reported an even higher poverty rate—83 percent—among a sample of recipients remaining on welfare for six months. Mean and median household incomes of ongoing recipients also were lower ($890 and $642, respectively) than those of former recipients. Although the Washington State study does not track the same group of people over time, it provides some evidence that economic status improves after exit from welfare.

In contrast, based on a longitudinal analysis of administrative data, Cancian, Haveman, Meyer, and Wolfe (2000) estimate that annualized income fell by over $2,000 among those leaving welfare in Wisconsin in 1995. Strong increases in earnings and estimates of the EITC were more

Table 3.3. Total Household Income and Percentage of Household Income Contributed by Various Sources

Grantee and Cohort*	Total Cash Income Mean (Median)	Own Earnings	Other's Earnings	AFDC /TANF	Child Support	SSI	Other Income
Arizona 98.1**	$1,338 (----)	45	40	3	3	5	3
Illinois 7/97–12/98	$946 ($800)						
Missouri 96.4	$1,427 ($1,166)	50	20	8	6	6	8
Wassington 98.4	$1,208 ($1,000)	55	28	8	7	1	1
Cuyahoga 98.3	$1,069 (----)	63	19	6	2	5	5
D. C. 98.4	$1,001 ($800)						
San Mateo 98.4	---- ($1,400)						

Note: Total cash income does not include the value of Food Stamps ($100 in Cuyahoga County and approximately $129 in Arizona). Income is based on survey questions about income from various sources, except in Illinois and Washington, D.C., where the survey asked only for total household income. Figures are for single-parent leavers, except that figures from Missouri and Washington, D.C., include small percentages of two-parent leavers, who generally have higher incomes.

*The numbers following the grantee name refer to dates. For example, "96.4" means cases existing in the fourth quarter of 1996.

**In Arizona, sources of income are based on a sample of leavers who include those who return to TANF after one month, as well as the traditional two-month leavers.

than offset by decreases in cash assistance and Food Stamps. The authors note, however, that their income measures are limited to the woman's own earnings and assistance and omit other potentially significant sources of household income.

In fact, according to survey data from five studies (see Table 3.3), the leavers' own earnings account for only 45 to 63 percent of total household cash income. Cash assistance from AFDC or TANF adds another 3 to 8 percent. Earnings of others in the household make up most of the remainder, accounting for 19 to 40 percent of total income. The final 9 to 20 percent of household income comes from child support payments, SSI, and other income, including social security and survivors' benefits, veterans' benefits, workers' compensation, and financial assistance from others.

These survey data caution against gauging economic status solely based on the leavers' earnings, TANF, and Food Stamp benefits. Administrative data therefore are of limited value for assessing total household resources. A major problem is the inability to link earnings and assistance records of others in the household. Survey data provide a better measure of household income, particularly if the survey questions probe for various sources of income.

Partly because of the challenges of measuring income, most leavers surveys also asked directly about economic hardship. According to six studies, relatively few leavers stayed at a homeless shelter after exit (1 to 4 percent, except one study estimated 17 percent). More leavers, however, reported utility cutoffs (12 to 36 percent), food shortages (13 to 52 percent), and an inability to get needed medical attention (8 to 31 percent).

Studies were split as to whether housing and food shortages were greater before or after exit; three found more hardship after exit, and three found less hardship after exit.[6] There was more consistency in the area of medical hardship; respondents in several states reported more difficulty getting needed medical care after exit from welfare. Finally, when directly asked about overall economic well-being, 46 to 68 percent of families in four states reported they were better off financially after exit, 16 to 30 percent said they were the same, and 13 to 30 percent said they were worse off.

Although the evidence is mixed, available information on income, poverty status, and material hardship suggests that the average leaver did not lose income after exit from welfare and in many cases was somewhat better off financially. Hardships remained, however. More than half were still in poverty, and many lacked access to health care.

Conclusion

This chapter examines how administrative and survey data can be combined to describe how leavers are faring. Administrative data provide information on patterns of employment and program participation over time and across states. For example, leavers' employment rates remained stable over the first four quarters after exit and were fairly consistent across states. In contrast, Medicaid participation declined during the first year after exit and varied significantly across states.

Survey data provide a fuller picture of how the leaver and her family are faring at the time of interview. They show, for example, that average household incomes were low, even when counting earnings from others in the household. Former recipients continued to experience some degree of material hardship, although not widespread homelessness. Survey data are often the only source of information on material hardships, child well-being, barriers to employment, attitudes toward welfare, and many other important topics not covered in this short overview.

In addition to demonstrating the complementary nature of administrative and survey data, this chapter has set the context for later chapters by describing typical outcomes for leavers across fourteen different states and counties. The chapters that follow move the research forward by analyzing a wider range of outcomes and examining outcomes among key subgroups.

Notes

1. The fourteen grantees were Arizona, District of Columbia, Florida, Georgia, Illinois, Massachusetts, Missouri, New York, South Carolina, Washington, Wisconsin, Cuyahoga County (Ohio), Los Angeles County, and a consortium of San Mateo, Santa Clara, and Santa Cruz counties in California. Included in this volume are results from studies in Arizona, Georgia, Illinois, and Missouri.

2. Final survey sample size varied from 277 to over 3,500 cases, and response rates generally ranged from 51 to 81 percent, with one study at 23 percent. Time of interview varied from six to thirty months after exit.

3. Although this volume focuses on families leaving welfare, many HHS-funded grantees also studied families applying for and diverted from welfare.

4. Recidivism was generally lower in studies that measured it on a monthly basis than in those that observed welfare receipt over a quarterly (three-month) period.

5. The potential for measurement variation can be seen in the fact that two studies more than doubled their initial enrollment rates from administrative data. In both cases, researchers reanalyzed administrative data and classified additional eligibility codes as Medicaid enrollment, after noting large discrepancies between administrative and survey data.

6. Two of the studies finding greater hardship after exit directly compared leavers with a group remaining on the rolls. (The other four studies asked leavers to try to recall their own experiences before and after exit). One leaver-recipient comparison study (Washington State) found both higher monthly incomes and more hardships among leavers, suggesting that material well-being may be affected by factors other than income (such as work expenses, noncash assistance, or income instability).

References

The material in this chapter draws on the following studies of families leaving welfare.

Acs, G., and Loprest, P. *The Status of TANF Leavers in the District of Columbia: Final Report.* Washington, D.C.: Urban Institute, Dec. 2000.

Acs, G., and Loprest, P. *Initial Synthesis Report of the Findings from ASPE'S "Leavers" Grants.* Washington, D.C.: Urban Institute, Jan. 2001.

Ahn, J., and others. *A Study of Washington State TANF Departures and Welfare Reform: Welfare Reform and Findings from Administrative Data.* Olympia: Washington Department of Social and Health Services, Feb. 2000.

Bross, N. *Employment, Earnings, and Recidivism Among Georgia's TANF Leavers.* Atlanta: Georgia Department of Human Resources, Jan. 2001.

Cancian, M., Haveman, R., Kaplan, T., and Wolfe, B. *Post-Exit Earnings and Benefit Receipt Among Those Who Left AFDC in Wisconsin.* Madison: Institute for Research on Poverty, University of Wisconsin-Madison, Jan. 1999.

Cancian, M., Haveman, R., Meyer, D., and Wolfe, B. *Before and After TANF: The Economic Well-Being of Women Leaving Welfare.* Madison: Institute for Research on Poverty, University of Wisconsin-Madison, May 2000.

Coulton, C., and Verma, N. *Monitoring Outcomes for Cuyahoga County's Welfare Leavers: How Are They Faring.* New York: Manpower Demonstration Research Corporation, Apr. 2001.

Crewe, R., Eyerman, J., Graham, J., and McMillan, N. *Tracking Outcomes of Welfare Reform in Florida for Three Groups of People*. Tallahassee: Florida State University, Oct. 2000.

Du, J., Fogarty, D., Hopps, D., and Hu, J. *A Study of Washington State TANF Leavers and TANF Recipients. Findings from the April-June 1999 Telephone Survey*. Olympia: Washington Department of Social and Health Services, Feb. 2000.

Foster, E. M., and Rickman, D. *Life After Welfare: Report of the Georgia Welfare Leavers Study*. Atlanta: Georgia State University, Jan. 2000.

Isaacs, J., and Lyon, M. "A Cross-State Examination of Families Leaving Welfare: Findings from the ASPE-Funded Leavers Studies." Paper presented at the National Association for Welfare Research and Statistics, Aug. 2000.

Julnes, G., and others. *Illinois Study of Former TANF Clients, Final Report*. Springfield: University of Illinois, Aug. 2000.

Massachusetts Department of Transitional Assistance. *After Time Limits: A Study of Household Leaving Welfare Between December 1998 and April 1999*. Boston: Massachusetts Department of Transitional Assistance. Nov. 2000.

Midwest Research Institute. *Economic Outcomes of Former Missouri AFDC Recipients: 1996 Cohort*. Kansas City: Midwest Research Institute, July 2001.

Moses, A., and Macuso, D. C. *Examining Circumstances of Individuals and Families Who Leave TANF: Assessing the Validity of Administrative Data*. Burlingame, Calif.: SPHERE Institute, Dec. 2000.

Richardson, P., and others. *Welfare Leavers and Diverters Research Study: One-Year Follow Up of Welfare Leavers*. Washington, D.C.: Maximus, Mar. 2001.

Ryan, S. *Preliminary Outcomes for 1996 Fourth Quarter AFDC Leavers: Revised Interim Report*. Columbia: University of Missouri-Columbia, Sept. 1999.

Rockefeller Institute, New York State Office of Temporary and Disability Assistance, and New York State Department of Labor. *After Welfare: A Study of Work and Benefit Use After Case Closing*. Albany: Rockefeller Institute, New York State Office of Temporary and Disability Assistance, and the New York State Department of Labor, Dec. 1999.

Westra, K., and Routley, J. *Arizona Cash Assistance Exit Study: First Quarter 1998 Final Report*. Phoenix: Arizona Department of Economic Security, Jan. 2000.

JULIA B. ISAACS is director of the Division of Data and Technical Analysis, Office of the Assistant Secretary for Planning and Evaluation, U.S. Department of Health and Human Services.

4

With an interest in supporting the existing social capacities of leavers of Temporary Assistance to Needy Families (TANF), this chapter incorporates psychosocial factors into a structural equation model that includes the outcomes of post-exit employment and TANF recidivism.

Understanding Self-Sufficiency of Welfare Leavers in Illinois: Elaborating Models with Psychosocial Factors

George Julnes, Xitao Fan, Kentaro Hayashi

The Personal Responsibility and Work Opportunity Reconciliation Act of 1996 (PRWORA) represented a major shift in the basic contract between the government and those in need of welfare support. Replacing the income maintenance entitlement of the Aid to Families with Dependent Children program (AFDC), the Temporary Assistance to Needy Families program (TANF) emphasized time-limited income support coupled with rapid attachment to the labor force. Primary goals of this legislation were to reduce welfare dependency and increase economic self-sufficiency.

Evaluation can support these goals by providing insights into the factors that influence dependency and self-sufficiency, but the insights derived will always be conditioned by how the task is approached. To the extent that particular evaluation approaches dominate the welfare reform literature, we limit unnecessarily the contributions that evaluation can make. This chapter presents research that complements the economic analyses of welfare reform (for example, analyses of the consequences for welfare participation

The analyses described in this chapter were conducted on the basis of a cooperative agreement with the Illinois Department of Human Services and the U.S. Department of Health and Human Services (grant 98ASPEC298A). The opinions and conclusions expressed here, however, are solely the authors' and should not be interpreted as reflecting the opinions and policies of the federal government or the state of Illinois.

We acknowledge those who reviewed earlier drafts of this chapter, in particular Steven Anderson and Patria de Lancer Julnes.

of an earned income tax credit or of low unemployment rates) with analyses of survey responses of people who have left welfare in Illinois. The goal is to elaborate our understanding of the factors that influence welfare dependency and self-sufficiency by incorporating psychological and social factors from the perspectives of the former TANF clients into our models. Given the complexity of the relationships between and among psychosocial factors, a second feature of this research is the use of structural equation modeling to depict the paths by which these outcomes are related to the prior factors. The basic argument is that it is important to incorporate these factors into our evaluations if we want the evaluations to provide the most useful guidance for policy reform.

Elaborating Models of Welfare Outcomes

A persistent debate in evaluation is the degree to which it is important or useful to develop a sophisticated understanding of the dynamics of what is being evaluated (Chen and Rossi, 1983; Scriven, 1997; Shadish, Cook, and Leviton, 1991). Pragmatic concerns include the costs of developing that understanding and the degree to which the policymaking process is improved by being so informed. In assessing the potential value of better understanding in our context, it is significant that despite the apparent success of welfare reform, there are reasons to be skeptical about whether the observed caseload reductions justify judging welfare reform a success (Tweedie, 2000). For example, there is evidence to suggest that even some who remain employed and off public assistance are struggling and not self-sufficient in any meaningful sense (Eitzen and Zinn, 2000; Green, 2000; Mink, 1998; Young, 2000). In addition, recidivism rates for returns to TANF have been relatively high even in the context of low unemployment, and many have questioned what will happen when the economy slows and demand for low-skill employees decreases (Besharov and Germanis, 2000; Ziliak, Figlio, and Davis, 2000).

These concerns argue for building on prior analyses of the factors that enhance post-welfare self-sufficiency (Bane and Ellwood, 1994) by incorporating the perspectives of leavers to yield a more finely grained understanding of the dynamics that promote positive outcomes. The outlines of such an understanding are beginning to take shape and guide the model development explored in this chapter. For example, lack of available child care has received considerable attention as a barrier that interferes with single parents' seeking and retaining jobs (Lino, 1998; Meyers, 1997). Including this factor in our understanding of TANF outcomes, however, requires knowing something of the needs of the TANF leavers (for example, whether other family members or friends are available to provide care) and not merely administrative information about program participation. Developing this example further, it is not just whether child care providers are available and affordable but also whether the care is available during the hours that the TANF leavers need to work (Presser and Cox, 1997; Westra, Chapter Ten, this volume).

Another factor that requires input from the leavers' perspectives is the nature of their relationships with spouses or partners. With influences ranging from domestic violence to more subtle discouragement and lack of support, many scholars have identified relationship problems as a challenge to state-sponsored efforts to improve the self-sufficiency of TANF clients and leavers (Danziger, Kalil, and Anderson, 1998; Hetling, 2000; Jayakody, Danziger, and Pollack, 2000). There is a potential for this relationship to operate in both directions, however; some have argued that improved economic self-sufficiency helps women leave violent relationships (Farmer and Tiefenthaler, 1997). Presumably other resources, such as social support from other sources, would also make it less likely for the leavers to experience relationship barriers to positive post-TANF outcomes.

These two factors point to a more general third factor: the degree to which leavers have friends or relatives who can provide informal social support. Building on previous findings on the importance of strong families and other forms of social support (Dodson, 1998; Edlin and Lein, 1997; Jarrett, 1994; Stack, 1974), TANF outcomes may be quite dependent on whether leavers have others who can help with daily tasks (for example, being able to watch the children while the mother does errands) or even provide resources (by loaning a car or money, perhaps). Described in this way, this more general factor is also expected to be an influence on whether TANF leavers have unmet child care needs and on the types of relationship barriers that these leavers might be experiencing.

In addition to these three influences on TANF outcomes, policymaking might also be improved by understanding more about the nature of TANF outcomes themselves. Specifically, we tend to presume that reduced welfare dependency and increased self-sufficiency are appropriate goals of welfare reform. However, when these goals are measured solely in terms of TANF recidivism and post-TANF employment, the well-being of both parents and children may be compromised by moving single parents off welfare rolls (Baratz and White, 1996; Mink, 1998). For example, some have noted that the state's interest in managerial efficiency (low recidivism and high work effort of leavers) often conflicts with an interest in welfare client and leaver well-being (Schram, 1995). While there are a variety of ways to measure well-being (Ringen, 1997), it would be useful to understand well-being from the perspectives of TANF leavers and relate this to the other TANF outcomes of recidivism and post-TANF employment.

In sum, we have argued for the importance of incorporating factors drawn from the perspectives of TANF leavers in developing our understanding of how to promote positive post-TANF outcomes (Danziger and Lin, 2000). Although much of the research involving the perspectives of TANF clients and leavers has been pioneered by qualitative researchers, quantitative techniques can be illuminating as well. The claim that this illumination is of value depends on the extent to which we benefit from having policy decisions made in the context of this understanding. In what follows, we report on a study that integrates information from a survey of TANF leavers in Illinois with administrative data on these leavers and uses structural equation modeling to relate the three explanatory factors to post-TANF outcomes, including a consideration of post-TANF well-being as reported by the leavers.

Illinois Study of Welfare Leavers

In 1998, the Illinois Department of Human Services (IDHS) cosponsored with the office of the Assistant Secretary of Program Evaluation, a division of the U.S. Department of Health and Human Services, a study of what was happening to people whose TANF cases were being closed. The study used both administrative and survey data to examine employment, economic, and subjective measures of post-TANF well-being.

Data. Administrative data used for this analysis were derived primarily from the IDHS client database (CDB), with quarterly wage information provided by the Illinois Department of Employment Security (IDES) quarterly wage file. The population of interest for the analyses of administrative data was all cases that closed between June 1997 and December 1998, the first eighteen months of TANF implementation in Illinois. A total of 124,819 single-parent cases and 12,511 two-parent cases (summing to the total of 137,330 first-exit cases) closed at least once during the study period. Variables available in the administrative data set include demographic information (such as education and age) of the adult identified as primary on the case, as well as case-level information (such as number of children on the case, Food Stamp and Medicaid services, and reason for case closure).

Survey data came from interviews conducted with a cohort of adults who had left TANF cash assistance in December 1998. From a sample of 1,001 adults (500 from the Chicago–Cook County area and 501 from a proportional sample of thirty-two other Illinois counties), 514 were located and interview by telephone.[1] The areas covered included reasons for leaving TANF, reasons for recidivism when applicable, details on job history both before and after leaving TANF, household income, support services received, and reasons for not receiving services when applicable. Also included were a variety of questions addressing psychosocial issues: degree of informal support, relationship problems, child care needs, hardships experienced before and after exit, satisfaction with different aspects of their lives, and overall assessment of whether aspects of their lives were better or worse since leaving TANF.

Previous Analyses. Descriptive analyses revealed that 22.8 percent of all leavers (137,300) had returned to TANF cash assistance at some point with six months of their first exit in the study period (exit refers to the first exit in the eighteen-month study period; some had previous welfare spells that closed prior to the study and some exited multiple times during the study; see Julnes and others, 2000). Looking at the other outcome variable, most leavers were employed at exit (54.9 percent of the 137,330 leavers were employed in the quarter of exit) and at interview (63.2 percent of the 514 interviewed).

To understand the dynamics responsible for these outcomes, logistic regression (Hosmer and Lemeshow, 1989) was used with the administrative data to identify predictor variables associated with recidivism and employment for TANF leavers. Results indicated that for single-parent cases headed by a female (representing the large majority of welfare cases in Illinois), a variety of factors were associated with increased recidivism within six months of exit. First, the employment and education experiences were important, with those having no prior work experience and no high school diploma being more likely to return to TANF. Second, younger clients, those never married, and those who were African American were more likely to return to TANF. Finally, those whose cases were closed for noncooperation reasons were approximately twice as likely to return to TANF as those whose cases closed for earned income–related reasons.

Factors associated with employment in the first quarter after exit (that is, having any wages reported in the unemployment insurance file for that quarter) for single-parent cases headed by a female were similar to those that predicted recidivism, but with some differences. Education and work experience were still important in predicting this outcome, as was the geo-economic region (the Chicago–Cook County region and the rural south of the state still having the worst outcomes). However, African Americans were equally as likely as white leavers to be employed, and younger clients, particularly when comparing those between seventeen and twenty-five years old with those older than age thirty, were more likely to be employed. Furthermore, in contrast with their higher recidivism, those never married were more likely to be employed after exit.

These analyses provided some insights into the factors associated with post-TANF self-sufficiency. The next step involved elaborating the models by incorporating the psychosocial factors that might be responsible for some of the patterns seen in these analyses of administrative data.

Methodology

Several aspects of the methodology used were described above. We address here the structural equation modeling (SEM) analyses that were used and the way that the model was developed using SEM.

SEM was developed in the late 1960s and early 1970s as an extension to factor analysis (see Joreskog and Sorbom, 1996). It analyzes the complex interrelations among posited psychological constructs (so-called factors), as well as observed variables (Bollen, 1989; Maruyama, 1998; Loehlin, 1998; Raykov and Marcoulides, 2000). Software packages available to analyze data using SEM include EQS (Bentler, 1995; Bentler and Wu, 1995), LISREL (Joreskog and Sorbom, 1996), Amos (Arbuckle and Wothke, 1999), and Mplus (Muthen and Muthen, 1998).

When using SEM, one begins with either an initial model or with competing models and then evaluates the model for fit with the data. These models differ in terms of the relationships that they specify among the underlying constructs or between the constructs and the available measures of those constructs. The degree of fit between a model and data is taken as evidence for the adequacy of the model and is evaluated using a variety of indices that have been developed for this purpose. There is no clear consensus on which of these indices provides a better measurement of fit, but one receiving considerable attention in recent years is the root mean square error of approximation (RMSEA) measure (Steiger and Lind, 1980; Browne and Cudeck, 1993). We used this index in conjunction with the goodness-of-fit index (GFI) and the adjusted goodness-of-fit index (AGFI). The RMSEA measure indicates excellent fit with values close to 0, preferably under 0.05; the other indices mentioned suggest an excellent fit of the model when they are close to 1. When the model fit can be improved, two optional tests in EQS, the Wald test and the Lagrange multiplier (LM) test, suggest how to modify the current model by either deleting some paths (Wald test) or adding paths (LM test).

Model Development

In accordance with the research questions we have set out, we employed SEM to study how three important outcomes for welfare reform—employment, recidivism, and client well-being—are related to each other and are explained by psychosocial and demographic risk factors. These explanatory factors are Social Support, Relationship Barriers, Child Care Needs, and a demographic at-risk factor, each with multiple measures (see Table 4.1). Two of the outcomes, Well-Being and Employment, were represented as factors, but Recidivism was measured as a single observed variable (former clients either returned to TANF cash assistance within six months of exit or did not). For clarity, we maintained a pure and simple structure; that is, we did not allow any observed variables to load on more than one factor. Observations with any missing values were deleted listwise, resulting in analyses with the data from 365 survey respondents being used.

Results

The initial runs of EQS were followed by the modification of the model based on the results of the multivariate LM tests and Wald tests. The final EQS model presented no special problems reaching the convergence. The average absolute standardized residuals was 0.0464, and the average off-diagonal absolute standardized residuals was 0.0489. The distribution of standardized residuals was clean, concentrated around the center.

Table 4.1. Relationships of Factors and Indicators

Factor 1: Informal Support:	Path Coefficient	t
"How often do you have someone you can count on:"		
To run errands	0.613	11.773
To lend you money	0.688	13.601
To give you encouragement	0.614	11.798
To watch your kids	0.629	12.165
To lend you a car	0.741	14.967

Factor 2: Relationship Barriers	Path Coefficient	t
"In the past 12 months, did a spouse, partner, or former partner ever:"		
Prevent you from working or going to school	0.805	7.493
Try to discourage you from finding a job or working	0.794	7.465
Make you feel guilty about working	0.678	7.120
Refuse to help you with child care, transportation, etc.	0.606	6.836
Make it difficult for you to attend or complete programs	0.722	7.265
Harass you with phone calls at your job	0.582	6.724
Injure you?	0.583	6.727
Cause you to go to a shelter	0.429	5.799
Cause you to lose or quit your job	0.557	6.603
Not show up or arrive under the influence of alcohol/drugs	0.403	(fixed)

Factor 3: Child Care Needs	Path Coefficient	t
"Has _____ been a problem for you in getting or keeping a job?"		
Paying for child care	0.673	9.529
Finding someone to take care of your children	0.815	10.566
Finding child care for the hours you needed to work	0.813	10.555
Getting your children to and from child care	0.569	(fixed)
Overall Question: "Any unmet child care needs?"	0.453	7.156

Factor 4: Risk Factors	Path Coefficient	t
High school diploma or more	−0.451	−4.433
No previous job experience	0.434	(fixed)
TANF case closed for Non-Cooperation	0.403	4.215
Live in Chicago/Cook County	0.453	4.440
Lifetime number of years on welfare	0.244	3.059

(Continued)

Table 4.1. *(Continued)*

Factor 5: Well Being	Path Coefficient	t
"How satisfied or dissatisfied you are with the following aspects of you life?" (1 = very satisfied; 2 = somewhat satisfied; 3 = somewhat dissatisfied; 4 = very dissatisfied)		
Your household's current financial situation	0.682	(fixed)
Your housing conditions	0.551	8.603
The quality of your relationship with your child	0.415	6.705
Your personal health and physical condition	0.510	8.052
The health and physical condition of your child	0.473	7.545
The quality of health care that you/family can afford	0.553	8.621
Your friendships	0.455	7.281

Factor 6: Employment	Path Coefficient	t
Monthly household income from any source	0.613	7.622
Non-Medicaid health insurance	0.478	6.592
Currently employed	0.540	7.143
Hourly pay	0.628	(fixed)

Several goodness-of-fit indices indicated a reasonable fit: GFI = 0.861, AGFI = 0.842, and CFI = 0.865. One reason that these values were not higher is likely the insistence on simple structure, where no observed variable (except for Recidivism, which was approached as an outcome factor) was allowed to contribute to factors other than the presumed construct that it was meant to measure. However, the value of RMSEA, at 0.047 (90 percent confidence interval from 0.043 to 0.052), indicated a very good fit and so strengthened confidence in this model.

Part of the success in having a well-fitting model was due to the observed variables having strong relationships with their specified factors. Table 4.1 presents these relationships in terms of estimated standardized path coefficients and the associated t-values that came from the unstandardized analysis. Most of the t-values are quite large, suggesting the strength and stability of the paths.

Figure 4.1 depicts the relationships among the factors (reporting the standardized path coefficients with the t-values from the unstandardized analyses in parentheses), including the variable Recidivism. As can be seen from Figure 4.1, Employment has a negative effect on Recidivism (−.213), indicating that those who are employed are less likely to return to welfare

Figure 4.1. Influence of Psychosocial Factors on TANF Outcomes

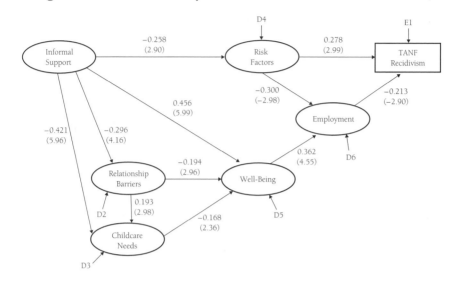

assistance. Risk Factors has positive effect on Recidivism (.278); that is, those with a higher score on Risk Factors are more likely to return to welfare assistance. Both of these make good sense. Risk Factors also has negative effect on Employment (–.30), meaning that those who have higher scores on Risk Factors tend to be less likely to be employed. So Risk Factors has not only a direct effect on Recidivism but also an indirect effect on Recidivism via Employment. The effects of Social Support on the four other factors are all positive and moderate (.421 to Child Care Needs, .296 to Relationship Barriers, .456 to Well-Being, and .258 to Risk Factors). The effect from Social Support to Well-Being is reasonably strong (.456), while Well-Being positively influences Employment. These relationships suggest the importance of social support on the desirable individual and social outcomes (Well-Being, Employment, and less Recidivism).

Conclusion

The goal of this research was to enhance our understanding of the factors responsible for positive post-welfare outcomes by examining the relationships among standard outcome constructs and the role of psychosocial factors in explaining these outcomes. One notable result was that the well-being construct, while naturally thought of as being affected by low recidivism and high employment, was found instead to be a predictor of those two outcomes. That is, recognizing the limits of establishing causality from survey data, self-reported well-being appears to be at least as much of a precursor as an effect of the other desired outcomes of employment and nonrecidivism. A second finding was that it appears difficult to overestimate the importance of informal social support as a factor responsible for positive post-welfare outcomes. Although many factors and variables were examined in developing the model presented in Figure 4.1, social support was always the predominant explanatory factor, in this model affecting well-being directly and having several indirect paths to each of the three desired outcomes.

What are we to make of these findings with regard to policy? Although the arena of psychological and social factors may be more complex than a sole focus on participation in public programs, there are some straightforward implications that need to be considered. First, these findings, in concert with those reported by Anderson, Halter, and Schuldt (Chapter Eight, this volume) and by Julnes, Hayashi, and Anderson (Chapter Seven, this volume), highlight the problem of a group of leavers who are isolated from any form of support. At the very least, such findings make it important for state agencies to improve their screening practices for potential eligibility for support services before cases are closed. This would also be the time to make arrangements for child care services—either processing for state subsidies or ensuring that there are friends or family members who can provide the services. Such screening efforts are consistent with the strength-based approach to social work wherein practice emphasizes building on existing client or community capacities (Chapin, 1995; Saleeby, 1997). More generally, our findings of the importance of social support are suggestive of the need to focus on social systems when thinking about welfare reform. For example, Bauer, Braun, and Olson (2000) argue that a systems approach is needed to move welfare policies away from a narrowly conceived notion of self-sufficient individuals to one of healthy families and communities. Others have emphasized the value of community-based approaches to human service delivery (Wolch, 1996). As with the strength-based approach, one value of these approaches is the importance they give to building on the existing capacities of the families and communities of TANF clients. There will, of course, be limits to the degree to which the necessary capacities are available, but these approaches reflect increased interest in developing social policies that work to develop these capacities.

Welfare policy has changed considerably in the past decade, and this evolution is likely to continue. We have presented results of research that support efforts to broaden the dialogue that guides this evolution. Rather than focusing solely on administrative outcomes such as employment and recidivism and predictor variables such as education and length of time on welfare, we have shown that incorporating such psychosocial factors as informal social support, relationship problems, and child care needs can suggest important insights with implications for more informed policy-making in support of strengthening employment outcomes and reducing recidivism.

Note

1. The survey is available at ipa.uis.edu/published_rpts.htm.

References

Arbuckle, J. L., and Wothke, W. *Amos 4.0 User's Guide.* Chicago: SmallWaters Corporation, 1999.

Bane, M. J., and Ellwood, D. T. "Increasing Self-Sufficiency by Reforming Welfare." In M. J. Bane and D. T. Ellwood (eds.), *Welfare Realities: From Rhetoric to Reform.* Cambridge, Mass.: Harvard University Press, 1994.

Baratz, M. S., and White, S. B. "Childfare: A New Direction for Welfare Reform." *Urban Studies,* 1996, *33,* 1935–1944.

Bauer, J. W., Braun, B., and Olson, P. D. "Welfare to Well-Being Framework for Research, Education, and Outreach." *Journal of Consumer Affairs,* 2000, *34,* 62–81.

Bentler, P. M. *EQS Structural Equations Program Manual.* (3rd ed.) Encino, Calif.: Multivariate Software, 1995.

Bentler, P. M., and Wu, E.J.C. *EQS for the Windows User's Guide.* Encino, Calif.: Multivariate Software, 1995.

Besharov, D. J., and Germanis, P. "Welfare Reform—Four Years Later." *Public Interest,* 2000, *140,* 17–35.

Bollen, K. A. *Structural Equations with Latent Variables.* New York: Wiley, 1989.

Browne, M. W., and Cudeck, R. "Alternative Ways of Assessing Model Fit." In K. Bollen and J. S. Long (eds.), *Testing Structural Equation Models.* Thousand Oaks, Calif.: Sage, 1993.

Chapin, R. K. "Social Policy Development: The Strengths Perspective." *Social Work,* 1995, *40,* 506–514.

Chen, H-T., and Rossi, P. H. "Evaluating with Sense: The Theory-Driven Approach." *Evaluation Review,* 1983, *7,* 283–302.

Danziger, S. K., Kalil, A., and Anderson, N. J. "Human Capital, Health and Mental Health of Welfare Recipients: Co-Occurrence and Correlates." *Journal of Social Issues,* 1998, *54,* 637–656.

Danziger, S., and Lin, A. C. (eds.). *Coping with Poverty: The Social Contexts of Neighborhood, Work, and Family in the African-American Community.* Ann Arbor: University of Michigan Press, 2000.

Dodson, L. *Don't Call Us Out of Name: The Untold Lives of Women and Girls in Poor America.* Boston: Beacon Press, 1998.

Edin, K., and Lein, L. *Making Ends Meet.* New York: Russell Sage Foundation, 1997.

Eitzen, D. S., and Zinn, M. B. "The Missing Safety Net and Families: A Progressive Critique of the New Welfare Legislation." *Journal of Sociology and Social Welfare,* 2000, *27,* 53–72.

Farmer, A., and Tiefenthaler, J. "An Economic Analysis of Domestic Violence." *Review of Social Economy,* 1997, *55,* 337–358.

Green, J. "Tough Sanctions, Tough Luck." *American Prospect,* 2000, *11,* 38.

Hetling, A. H. "Addressing Domestic Violence as a Barrier to Self-Sufficiency: The Relationship of Welfare Receipt and Spousal Abuse." *Journal of Public and International Affairs,* 2000, *11,* 21–35.

Hosmer, D. W., and Lemeshow, S. *Applied Logistic Regression.* New York: Wiley, 1989.

Jarrett, R. L. "Living Poor: Family Life Among Single Parent, African-American Women." *Social Problems,* 1994, *41,* 30–49.

Jayakody, R., Danziger, S. H., and Pollack, H. "Welfare Reform, Substance Use, and Mental Health." *Journal of Health Politics, Policy, and Law,* 2000, *25,* 623–651.

Joreskog, K. G. "A General Method for Analysis of Covariance Structures." *Biometrika,* 1970, *57,* 239–251.

Joreskog, K., and Sorbom, D. *Lisrel 8: User's Reference Guide.* Chicago: Scientific Software International, 1996.

Julnes, G., and others. Illinois Study of Former TANF Clients, Final Report. Springfield: University of Illinois for the Illinois Department of Human Services, Aug. 2000.

Lino, M. "Child Care and Welfare Reform." *Family Economics and Nutrition Review,* 1998, *11,* 41–48.

Loehlin, J. C. *Latent Variable Models: An Introduction to Factor, Path, and Structural Analysis.* (3rd ed.) Hillside, N.J.: Erlbaum, 1998.

Maruyama, G. M. *Basics of Structural Equation Modeling.* Thousand Oaks, Calif.: Sage, 1998.

Meyers, M. K. "Child Day Care in Welfare Reform: Are We Targeting Too Narrowly?" *Child Welfare,* 1995, *74,* 33–52.

Mink, G. *Welfare's End.* Ithaca, N.Y.: Cornell University Press, 1998.

Muthen, L. K., and Muthen, B. O. *Mplus: The Comprehensive Modeling Program for Applied Researchers: User's Guide.* Los Angeles: Muthen and Muthen, 1998.

Presser, H. B., and Cox, A. G. "The Work Schedules of Low-Educated American Women and Welfare Reform." *Monthly Labor Review,* 1997, *120,* 25–34.

Raykov, T., and Marcoulides, G. A. *A First Course in Structural Equation Modeling.* Hillside, N.J.: Erlbaum, 2000.

Ringen, S. *Citizens, Families, and Reform.* New York: Oxford University Press, 1997.

Saleeby, D. (ed.). *The Strengths Perspective in Social Work Practice.* White Plains, N.Y.: Longman, 1997.

Schram, S. F. *Words of Welfare: The Poverty of Social Science and the Social Science of Poverty.* Minneapolis: University of Minnesota Press, 1995.

Scriven, M. S. "Minimalist Theory: The Least Theory That Practice Requires." *American Journal of Evaluation,* 1997, *19,* 57–70.

Shadish, W. R., Cook, T. D., and Leviton, L. C. *Foundations of Program Evaluation: Theories of Practice.* Thousand Oaks, Calif.: Sage, 1991.

Stack, C. B. *All Our Kin: Strategies for Survival in a Black Community.* New York: Harper-Collins, 1974.

Steiger, J. H., and Lind, J. C. "Statistically Based Tests for the Number of Common Factors." Paper presented at the Annual Meeting of the Psychometric Society, Iowa, 1980.

Tweedie, J. "From D.C. to Little Rock: Welfare Reform at Mid-Term." *Publius,* 2000, *30,* 69–97.

Wolch, J. R. Community-Based Human Service Delivery. *Housing Policy Debate,* 1996, *7,* 649–671.

Young, I. "New Disciplines of Work and Welfare." *Dissent,* 2000, *47,* 25–30.

Ziliak, J. P., Figlio, D. N., and Davis, E. E. "Accounting for the Decline in AFDC Caseloads: Welfare Reform or the Economy?" *Journal of Human Resources,* 2000, *35,* 570–586.

George Julnes is assistant professor of psychology with the Research and Evaluation Methodology Program and director of the Center for Policy and Program Evaluation at Utah State University.

Xitao Fan is associate professor in the Curry School of Education at the University of Virginia.

Kentaro Hayashi is assistant professor of psychology with the Research and Evaluation Methodology Program and senior researcher in the Center for Policy and Program Evaluation at Utah State University.

5

Using administrative and survey data from Georgia, this chapter examines the risk factors for recidivism among welfare leavers and the relationship between recidivism and leavers' ability to find sustained employment.

Patterns of Recidivism for Welfare Leavers

Dana K. Rickman, Nancy Bross, E. Michael Foster

The Personal Responsibility and Work Opportunity Reconciliation Act of 1996 (PRWORA) embodies a work-first strategy for moving families off welfare and toward self-sufficiency. What had been an entitlement became a limited resource on which families could draw during an emergency. The expectation that parents should work to support their families is now communicated to recipients and supported through program requirements and a mix of incentives and sanctions.

Under PRWORA, the Temporary Assistance for Needy Families (TANF) caseloads in Georgia have plummeted. Between January 1997 and January 2000, the number of families receiving TANF in Georgia dropped by more than 63,000, representing nearly a 55 percent reduction in three years. By this narrow standard, welfare reform has been a success. However, a fuller assessment would reflect an understanding of the extent to which former recipients subsequently return to the rolls and are able to find and keep good jobs.

To answer these questions, the state of Georgia funded two projects that combined the low cost and efficiency of population archival data with the greater depths of information offered by sample surveys. Using these data, this chapter examines recidivism and the factors that determine which leavers return to the rolls. It also explores the relationship between earnings and recidivism over time and how these relationships may evolve as families remain off the rolls.

We thank the Georgia Department of Human Resources, Division of Family and Children Services, and the U.S. Department of Health and Human Services, Assistant Secretary for Planning and Evaluation, for the funding for the work reported in this chapter.

Background

Prior research from academic studies of existing data provides some insight into the extent of and risk factors for recidivism, as well as the relationship between employment and recidivism. We then consider a second body of literature that examines the link between employment and welfare receipt.

Using data from the Panel Study of Income Dynamics (PSID) for the years 1983 through 1988, Harris (1996) examined the process by which single mothers who ever experienced and ended a spell on welfare returned to welfare. First, Harris described patterns of returns to welfare by number of spells and route of exit. Then she employed event history models to identify the timing and determinants of repeat dependency. She found that rates of return were high in the first year following an exit from welfare but declined subsequently. Once a woman remained off welfare for two years or more, the chances of repeat dependency dropped dramatically. Harris concluded that the most important factors influencing repeat dependency were a woman's earnings and factors that determined her economic security: education, number of children, age, and marriage or cohabitation with a working partner. Women who remained off welfare following their first exit were those with more human capital and fewer family responsibilities and who were less isolated in an urban center. Among those leaving for employment, women with low wages or unstable jobs were most likely to return to the rolls. Women who were able to find stable jobs were less likely to return than even those who exited for marriage.

Building on Harris (1996), Boisjoly, Harris, and Duncan (1998) examined twenty-eight years of PSID data using event history methods; they considered trends in the number and duration of welfare spells and the events and demographic characteristics associated with their initiation. The authors found that young age, low education levels, out-of-wedlock births, and a never-married status were all determinants of initial spells and duration of receipt. The most frequent characteristics of beginning spells included a lack of high school diploma, little or no previous work experience, being African American, and having a child under the age of three. Finally, the authors found that age at first birth (under age nineteen) and a never-married status were associated with the longest duration of welfare spells.

Relevant to this chapter, the authors associated the longest duration of spells with those who entered the rolls in the late 1980s, which the authors attributed to the recession of the early 1990s. The recession reduced the chance of exits due to employment. For those who did leave, that time period was also when real wages of low-skilled women began to fill. Although these authors' focus was on length of welfare spells, they also considered recidivism. The authors found that spells were longer and repeat dependency higher during times when recipients and former recipients were unable to sustain employment at high enough wages.

Blank (1989) examined individual spells of welfare, focusing on how the length of a spell affects the probability of its termination. She examined whether staying on the rolls for longer periods makes leaving welfare more difficult. However, her analyses also provided some insight into risk factors for repeat dependency. Using hazard modeling, Blank concluded that household composition was important in determining how quickly a woman would leave welfare. White women who were older when their spell began, with higher education levels, fewer children, and fewer young children, moved off the rolls faster. Taken together, these factors affect a women's economic status and ability to find and retain a job at higher wages. Women with these characteristics were also more likely to stay off welfare and not have repeat spells. Taken together, these works highlight the fact that it matters not only whether the woman finds a job but also what type of job she finds. This issue is directly addressed by the next study.

A second body of research focuses on the link between welfare receipt and employment. Using data from the National Longitudinal Survey of Youth (NLSY), Pavetti and Acs (1997) examined welfare use and the quality of employment: the transition from what they term a "bad job" to a "good job." The authors defined a good job as "one in which a woman usually works at least 35 hours a week and earns at least $8.00 per hour" (p. 1). This criterion translates roughly into earnings of $3,000 per quarter, or $12,000 a year, which is approximately the poverty threshold for a single parent with one child (U.S. Census Bureau, 2000). For larger families, earnings at this level would leave the family below the poverty line unless the family drew on additional sources of income. Among all women, the authors found that transitions from bad to good jobs were fairly common; those transitions, however, are far less common for the subgroups of women who ever used the welfare system for support. For this study, the authors did not consider repeat use of AFDC or TANF.

A substantial fraction of women spend time working in good jobs, and most of these women are established in these jobs by their late twenties. The authors found especially low probabilities of ever holding good jobs and of holding onto them steadily by their late twenties among women who had low levels of education, were African American, or had more than one child. Most important, few women who ever turned to the welfare system for support ever worked in good jobs (42 percent). Of those who did, only 13 percent worked steadily in good jobs.

Pavetti and Acs concluded that those who ever relied on welfare and those with characteristics identified by the literature of those at risk for recidivism (previous work, race, age, number of children) had very low possibilities of obtaining a good job and ever lower probabilities of sustaining a good job.

In sum, the studies consistently identify women who are at risk for repeat dependency: those with low education levels, who are young or have young children, who are African American, or who have never been married. In addition to demographic characteristics, the studies also linked the importance of having not only a job but also job quality, as defined by earnings.

Given these findings, our next step is to examine Georgia leavers. In order to put our results in a context, we next present the particularities of the TANF laws in Georgia.

TANF in Georgia

Several key features distinguish welfare reform in Georgia and affect the likelihood that welfare leavers will return to the rolls over time. First, the state has opted for a four-year time limit (one year less than the federal guidelines allow) with no exemptions based on caring for disabled persons (as allowed in some other states). Second, Georgia policy includes fairly strict employment standards and program guidelines. TANF recipients must sign both a personal responsibility contract and an employment contract. The personal responsibility contract requires participation in work activities, adherence to child school attendance requirements, participation in life skills or parenting classes, drug or alcohol provisions (if deemed necessary), and attendance at parent-teacher conferences. The applicant also must complete an employability plan that covers work requirements. The only applicants exempt from the employability plan are those with a child under age twelve months (Center for Law and Social Policy and the Center on Budget and Policy Priorities, 1999).

Third, benefits are lower in Georgia than in most other states. According to the U.S. Department of Health and Human Services, the average monthly benefit level for Georgians ($231) is considerably less than the national average ($357). Fourth, Georgia differs from some other states in how it defines eligibility. The state has eliminated the earnings disregard for working recipients. Recipients must have countable assets below $1,000. Comparatively, thirty states have asset limits between $2,000 and $3,000, and another six states have limits between $3,500 and $5,000. Unlike thirty-one other states, child-support payments are counted as income (Center for Law and Social Policy and the Center on Budget and Policy Priorities, 1999).

Finally, unlike some other states (one of them is Idaho), Georgia does pay larger amounts to larger families, but Georgia is among the minority of states that have imposed a strict family cap: welfare payments are not increased for women giving birth while on welfare after the case has been open for ten months.

Georgia TANF laws are designed to encourage work, and any type of work is viewed as an improvement to TANF. However, if earning levels are tied to a successful transition off, then policies that encourage obtaining just any job may not be sufficient.

State of Georgia Studies

Given the nearly 60 percent reduction in the TANF rolls, Georgia policy-makers felt it was necessary to track leavers in order to assess how many were either able to achieve sustained employment or were forced to return to the rolls. They also were interested in how these movements were related to broader measures of self-sufficiency and well-being. As a result, the state funded two projects: one using administrative data and the other an in-depth sample survey. The former provides information on employment and recidivism for the population of leavers; the latter provides a broader sense of how families are faring.

TANF Administrative Follow-Up Data. The TANF Administrative Follow-Up Data capture information on earnings and recidivism among TANF household heads following case closure. Included are 20,237 adults who left Georgia's TANF program during the last six months of 1997. The cohort of leavers included is somewhat dated because of data processing lags. A focus on these earlier cohorts also allows for longer follow-up periods.

All data in this file are derived from administrative data systems. Closed cases are identified using administrative data on welfare receipt. A case is considered closed when no cash benefits are received in two successive months. Only adults who were actually TANF recipients (included in the TANF grant) are included in this system. Excluded are adult heads of child-only cases and other adult household members not included in the TANF grant. Subsequent use of welfare is tracked using the active TANF case files from subsequent months.

Employment data are derived from the state unemployment insurance (UI) program and include earnings from UI-covered employment. Although over 90 percent of Georgia's workforce is covered under UI, the program does not cover self-employment, federal employment, employment in neighboring states, or informal employment taking place off the books. Consequently, these data represent a lower bound on total earnings.

Interview Data. While informative, administrative data are somewhat limited in scope. They provide no information on many key outcomes (such as a leaver's mental health or barriers to employment) and exclude some individuals, notably those no longer involved in any public programs and not working in covered employment. As a result, a second project was funded to conduct a telephone interview, covering a wide range of topics, with approximately two hundred leavers per month. Interviews were conducted between May 1999 and December 2000, approximately six months after exit from welfare.

All respondents completed a core set of items concerning demographics, employment, and economic status at the time of the interview. Individuals also completed a randomly chosen module. The module topics were sources of income and transportation, child care arrangements, mother's mental health and exposure to domestic violence, parenting and home environment, and understanding of welfare reform. Having study participants answer only part of the survey allowed us to include a wide range of topics in the interview without overburdening respondents. Because the data are missing at random (Schafer, 1997), conventional analytical methods easily allow for the resulting patterns of missing data.

Taken together, the administrative and survey data provided information on a range of key characteristics and outcomes and allow us to answer the questions of interest.

Results

We begin by presenting characteristics of the 1997 leavers in Georgia, summarized in Table 5.1. Unfortunately, data on length of time on TANF, education level, and marital status are not available for the 1997 cohort of leavers.[1] However, in subsequent cohorts, about 60 percent of leavers were high school graduates, and 70 percent had never married.

Risk Factors for Recidivism. First, we sought to determine the risk factors for recidivism. Table 5.2 shows employment, earnings, and recidivism in the two years following exit. Although information on why these leavers left TANF is not available, 63 percent had reported earnings for the quarter during which they left TANF. Over the following two years, employment rates declined gradually, leveling off at 58 percent in the fifth through eighth post-exit quarters. At the same time, average quarterly earnings among those who were employed increased, rising from $2,201 in the first post-exit quarter to $2,889 in the eighth. Recidivism was low, ranging from 6 percent to 14 percent and reaching a peak in the fourth and fifth quarters.

Table 5.1. Characteristics of 1997 Adult TANF Leavers

Female	96.4%
Average age	30.2
Racial group	
White	28.5%
African American	69.6%
Other	2.0%
County of residence	
Urban	34.9%
Suburban	27.3%
Rural	37.8%
Average number of dependent children	1.8
Average age of youngest child	5.6
Total N	20,237

Table 5.2. Employment and Recidivism of 1997 Adult TANF Leavers by Post-Exit Quarter

Post-Exit Quarter	Employment Rate	Average Earnings of Employed	Returned to TANF
1	63%	$2,201	6%
2	60%	$2,243	11%
3	59%	$2,393	13%
4	59%	$2,595	14%
5	59%	$2,553	14%
6	58%	$2,557	13%
7	58%	$2,722	12%
8	58%	$2,889	11%

Note: Median earnings were approximately $200 lower than average earnings across all quarters.

Table 5.2 makes it clear that the majority of leavers do not return to the rolls. What separates those who do? As shown in Table 5.3, those who returned were slightly younger, had slightly more children, were more likely to be a minority, and were more likely to live in either a rural or urban area. Perhaps surprisingly, those who return were only somewhat more likely to have been employed in the quarter they left TANF. For the comparison

Table 5.3. Leaver Characteristics and Recidivism in the Two Years Following Exit ($n = 20,237$)

	Outcomes in Two Years Following Exit		
Characteristic	Returned to TANF	Did Not Return	p value
Percentage of leavers*	26.9%	73.1%	
Average age	21.8	31.9	.001
Average number of children	2.9	2.7	.024
Average age of youngest child	4.7	5.9	.014
Employment rate in exit quarter	69.2%	63.4%	.001
White	31.9%	19.3%	.000
African American	65.8%	79.7%	
Other minority	2.3%	1%	
Urban	39.7%	33.2%	.000
Suburban	19.1%	30.4%	
Rural	41.2%	36.5%	

* Total N = 20,237.

groups, we provide statistical significance. In the case of continuous out-comes, we used the appropriate t-test for comparison of means. For cate-gorical outcomes, we used a chi-square test. As found in the previous studies, race and employment in exit quarter were highly significant. Also found significant were the age of the individual, the age and number of chil-dren in the home, and the region.

These data suggest that being employed is not enough to stay off TANF. One possibility is that many leavers are unable to maintain employment after exiting. Consistent with this explanation is the slow erosion of employment rates following exit. This possibility leads to our second topic.

Stable Employment for Former Recipients. While most leavers work in the quarter of exit, a key question is whether leavers are able to find stable employment. Table 5.4 shows the distribution of quarters employed. Only 18 percent of leavers never worked in the two years following. (Some of these individuals may have worked in noncovered employment, and so it is likely that nearly all leavers worked in some form of employment during this period.) At the same time, the table reveals substantial instability of employment; only one in three leavers left the rolls and worked in all eight quarters following exit.

Stability of employment is associated with but not equivalent to hav-ing a good job (as defined by Pavetti and Acs). Clearly, the relationship between stability of employment and earnings is strong. Average quarterly earnings for individuals working in every quarter are more than three times the quarterly earnings for individuals who worked in a single quarter. These differences in average earnings translate into differences in the percentage of workers with a good job. That percentage rises from 0 percent to 43 per-cent. Nonetheless, it is quite striking that the majority of leavers (57 per-cent) who work in every quarter following exit do not earn wages high enough to lift their families out of poverty.

Table 5.4. Average Quarterly Earnings and Total Earnings by Number of Quarters Employed over Two-Year Period
Total N = 20,237

Number of Quarters Employed	Percentage of Leavers	Average Quarterly Earnings in Quarters Employed	Average Two-Year Earnings	Percentage Level of with "Good Job" Income
0	18%	—	—	—
1	6%	$983	$983	0%
2	6%	$1,172	$2,343	1%
3	6%	$1,338	$4,014	1%
4	6%	$1,565	$6,261	4%
5	7%	$1,692	$8,463	6%
6	8%	$1,977	$11,862	10%
7	12%	$2,365	$16,552	20%
8	31%	$3,090	$24,719	43%

If a majority of welfare leavers are not able to maintain the good job standard but are continuing with sustained employment, are they also returning to welfare? We consider that question next.

The Relationship Between Recidivism and Earnings. Table 5.5 describes the relationship between stability of employment and return to TANF. This relationship is not linear. As expected, individuals who are employed in every quarter are least likely to return to the rolls; they are less than half as likely to return to the rolls as an individual who worked in half of the quarters (15.4 percent versus 42.4 percent, respectively). Furthermore, even when they do return to the rolls, they remain on the rolls for half as long (a median of ten versus four months).

Leavers who worked in every quarter are no less likely to return to the rolls than individuals who never worked (15.8 percent). This pattern suggests that to a substantial extent, earnings—or, at least, earnings in jobs covered under the UI system—did not account for why many leavers stayed off TANF. Other factors may have included marriage, relocation, dependence on family members, or receipt of disability payments.

Table 5.6 makes it clear that some leavers combine work and welfare—if not in the same quarter, then at some point after leaving the rolls initially. The relationship between employment and recidivism implies four groups of women: those who (1) are employed at some point but return to the rolls, (2) are employed and do not return, (3) are never employed and do return to the rolls, and (4) are never employed yet never return. Table 5.6 describes these four groups. The largest group of women (57.6 percent) comprises those who are employed and do not return to the rolls. The smallest group comprises those who are never employed and return to the rolls.

These data give a better understanding of the 24 percent of leavers in Table 5.6 for whom work and welfare were combined. Again, high significance levels were found for those who were younger, had younger children,

Table 5.5. Return to TANF by Quarters of Employment

Quarters of Employment	Returned to TANF*	Median Months on TANF**
0	15.8%	9
1	31.8%	10
2	37.1%	10
3	43.4%	10
4	42.2%	9
5	45.0%	8
6	39.1%	7
7	31.8%	6
8	15.4%	4

* N = 20,237.

**Includes only the 5,453 leavers who returned to TANF during the two-year period.

Table 5.6. Leaver Characteristics by Employment and Recidivism: Outcomes Two Years Following Exit

| | Outcomes in Two Years Following Exit | | | | | |
| | Ever Employed | | | Never Employed | | |
Characteristic	Returned to TANF	Did Not Return	p-value	Returned to TANF	Did Not Return	p-value
Percentage of leavers*	24.0%	57.6%		2.9%	15.5%	
Average age	27.5	30.1	.001	32.6	33.9	.003
Average number of children	1.9	1.8	.110	1.8	1.7	.114
Average age of youngest child	4.5	5.7	.002	6.4	7.2	.002
Employment rate in exit quarter	75.8%	77.5%	.026	14.9%	11.5%	.023
White	18.1%	29.9%	.000	29.6%	39.4%	.000
African American	81.0%	68.4%		68.9%	56.4%	
Other minority	.9%	1.7%		1.4%	4.2%	
Urban	40.1%	33.4%	.000	36.2%	32.4%	.000
Suburban	19.3%	30.4%		17.9%	30.5%	
Rural	40.6%	36.3%		45.8%	37.1%	

* Total N = 20,237.

were African American, and were living in either urban or rural counties. These leavers appear to have lacked both alternative forms of support and the level of earnings necessary to achieve sustained employment and independence from TANF.

The Use of Interview Data. Administrative data are informative but somewhat limited in scope. Interview data support what the administrative data reveal and can deepen our knowledge about what happens to individuals once they leave TANF.

Although the earnings of these leavers are low, only a small percentage are returning to TANF. Nine months after exit, only 18 percent of the leavers in the study had returned to TANF. How are they managing to stay off?

Table 5.7 shows that a majority of leavers were working at the time of the interview; however, only a small minority reported earnings consistent with the good job standard.

Leaving TANF does not mean an end to government assistance and self-sufficiency. The data in the TANF Administrative Follow-Up file do not tell us what mixture of government programs and nongovernment assistance are

Table 5.7. Interview Data on Self-Sufficiency

		Employed at Time of Interview	Reported "Good Job" Earnings
Marital status	Married	49%	38%
	Widowed	37%	12%
	Divorced	58%	30%
	Separated	61%	14%
	Never married	67%	16%
	Cohabitating	59%	22%
Age	Less than 18	66%	12%
	18–25	68%	15%
	25–35	67%	23%
	35–45	59%	19%
	Greater than 45	35%	19%
Race	White	51%	25%
	Nonwhite	63%	19%
Education levels	High school/ GED	68%	17%
	Less than high school	43%	11%
	Some college	68%	33%
Total N		2866	1540

being used by individuals who remain off TANF. According to the interview data, many households are managing to stay off welfare through a combination of other government programs and personal resources not reflected in the administrative data. As shown in Table 5.8, of those employed at exit, fewer than half (44 percent) reported having enough of the types and kinds of food they needed. To supplement that, 18 percent received additional food from their church, and 40 percent relied on friends and family. Moreover, 46 percent reported just breaking even every month, and 19 percent did not have enough money to cover their needs each month. To help make ends meet, 60 percent reported living in public housing, and 81 percent still received Medicaid.

Those who were not employed showed even lower levels of self-sufficiency. Only 39 percent reported having enough of the types and kinds of food they needed. Eighteen percent relied on their church for food and another 42 percent relied on friends and family. Twenty-eight percent reported there was not enough money to cover their expenses at the end of each month. Chi-square tests showed that those who were employed at exit were significantly more likely to have enough of the types and kinds of food they wanted and extra money at the end of the month.

In general, leavers report using a combination of existing government programs (other than TANF) and reliance on their family and friends to help sustain their transition off cash assistance. Those who are employed tend to be slightly better off. However, most of them are not employed at good job levels.

Table 5.8. Levels of Self-Sufficiency by Employment

	Employed at Exit	Not Employed at Exit	p-value
Have enough food of wanted types/kinds	44%	39%	.000
Receive needed food from church	18%	18%	.182
Receive needed food from friends and family	40%	42%	
Live in public housing	60%	57%	.270
Medicaid	81%	82%	.125
End of the month, some extra money	31%	20%	.023
End of the month, just breaking even	46%	43%	
End of the month, not enough money	19%	28%	
Total N	1866	1000	

Conclusion

The goal of the 1996 welfare reform laws was to change the culture of welfare dependency by moving people off welfare and into employment. Therefore, a secondary goal would be for former recipients to remain off welfare and move above the poverty level. The data indicate that there is a threshold of earnings (approximately $3,000) per quarter that former recipients need to survive at the poverty line. This threshold is also related to an individual's ability to sustain employment over multiple quarters, thereby decreasing the chance of a return welfare spell. However, sustained employment does not necessarily require a good job. In Georgia, only 43 percent of those who worked in all quarters had earnings in the eighth post-exit quarter that met the Pavetti and Acs's good job criterion of $3,640 a quarter. This finding should be generalizable to other states as well. Results from Georgia indicate that sustained employment may be the result of wages that fall below the poverty line. Moreover, sustained employment is one key to staying off TANF. Nevertheless, wages that approached the poverty line helped ensure continued employment quarter to quarter.

Former recipients in Georgia at risk for recidivism resemble other former recipients nationwide. Those at greater risk are younger, have more children, are less educated, and are African American. However, peculiarities of the Georgia TANF program allow these results to be generalizable to only a certain extent. For example, the four-year time limit had not gone into effect for the individuals included in this study. Subsequent cohorts of leavers began to hit the time limit in January 2001. Those approaching the four-year limit may leave by taking lower-paying jobs in an attempt to "save up" their months. These lower-paying jobs may actually increase their risk for recidivism. Therefore, a policy designed to move people off the rolls may actually encourage future use. Once recipients exceed their four-year limit, if they were continually working in lower-paying jobs, they may become even more dependent on other government programs such as Food Stamps and Medicaid.

It is evident that in order to move people off welfare government assistance successfully and permanently, policies need to be targeted at those who are likely to need the most help: those with low education levels, younger children, and low levels of employment experience. Policies aimed at simply finding any job may not be sufficient for sustained employment or even a permanent transition off TANF.

Note

1. Due to a transfer of management information systems for the TANF administrative database during 1997, archival data on length of time on TANF, education level, and marital status are available beginning only in 1998.

References

Blank, R. "Analyzing the Length of Welfare Spells." *Journal of Public Economics*, 1989, *39*, 245–273.

Boisjoly, J., Harris, K. M., and Duncan, G. J. 1998. "Trends, Events, and Duration of Welfare Spells." *Social Service Review*, Dec. 1998, pp. 466–492.

Center for Law and Social Policy and the Center on Budget and Policy Priorities. "State Policy Documentation Project." [www.spdp.org/index.htm]. 1999.

Harris, K. M. "Life After Welfare: Women, Work, and Repeat Dependency." *American Sociological Review*, 1996, *61*, 407–426.

Pavetti, L., and Acs, G. *Moving Up, Moving Out or Going Nowhere? A Study of the Employment Patterns of Young Women.* Washington, D.C.: Urban Institute, July 1997.

Schafer, J. L. *Analysis of Incomplete Multivariate Data.* New York: Chapman and Hall, 1997.

DANA K. RICKMAN *is a graduate student in the Department of Political Science and Research Associate at the Applied Research Center at Georgia State University.*

NANCY BROSS *is a private consultant in Atlanta, Georgia.*

E. MICHAEL FOSTER *is associate professor of health policy and administration at The Pennsylvania State University.*

6

Using administrative and survey data from Georgia, this chapter examines the status of children living in families leaving welfare.

Welfare Reform and Children: A Comparison of Leavers and Stayers in Georgia

Dana K. Rickman, E. Michael Foster

Critics of welfare have longed cited its negative effects on children. Aid to Families with Dependent Children (AFDC) was believed to worsen children's situations in a variety of ways, including encouraging the formation and maintenance of single-parent families. AFDC also was believed to shape children's long-term views of employment and idleness. Under that program, recipients were guaranteed lifetime benefits with no requirements to work or even to prepare for work. Therefore, children were being raised in homes that were heavily dependent on assistance for long periods of time. The lesson for children was that work was not the norm (Murray, 1999). From this view, the cycle of dependency was a direct result of cash assistance programs like AFDC.

These concerns helped lead to the Personal Responsibility and Work Opportunity Reconciliation Act of 1996 (PRWORA), which replaced AFDC with the Temporary Assistance for Needy Families (TANF) block grant. Various aspects of TANF were designed to improve the lives of children, including assistance to needy families so that children may be cared for in their own homes or in the homes of relatives. By extending aid to two-parent families, TANF also encourages the formation and maintenance of two-parent families. Perhaps most important, TANF seeks to move needy parents off government benefits and into employment by using work requirements, time limits, and participation in the personal responsibility program.

We thank the Georgia Department of Human Resources, Division of Family and Children Services, and the U.S. Department of Health and Human Services, Assistant Secretary for Planning and Evaluation, for the funding for the work reported in this chapter.

How are children faring under welfare reform? Available research on welfare leavers is growing rapidly but still fairly limited. Much of this research is based on the experiences of families leaving the old AFDC system or participating in various experimental programs. Relatively little is known about the children in families leaving welfare after the 1996 law.

Complicating efforts to understand the effect of welfare reform is heterogeneity among the TANF population. Among children, one source of such variation is the presence of adults in the case: whether the case is a child-only or single-parent case. In a child-only case, no adults are recipients. Although the size of the child-only caseload is shrinking, the rate of decrease is less than that for the single-parent caseload. As a result, child-only cases are growing as a proportion of the total caseload. In 1996, these cases made up 17 percent of the active caseload nationally. By 1998, this figure had risen to 23 percent (Lewin Group, 2000). In spite of these trends, virtually nothing is known about child-only cases. Indeed, most studies of welfare leavers exclude these cases.

Using recent data from Georgia, this chapter examines the status of children living in families leaving welfare. To put these figures in a context, we also provide data on a smaller sample of children living in families remaining on welfare. We used data from a Georgia study of leavers and from a parallel study of stayers, as well as administrative data from various sources. We use this information to describe the children themselves, as well as the adult outcomes that predict long-term child outcomes. Because so little is known about child-only cases, we present separate findings for children in child-only and single-parent cases. Disaggregating cases in this way often reveals striking differences between the two groups.

Framework for Evaluating the Effect on Children of Leaving Welfare

Figure 6.1 describes our conceptual framework for examining the impact of leaving welfare on children.[1] As the figure illustrates, there are two areas through which the reform laws can ultimately affect children. The first are the family structure regulations designed—at best—to promote two-parent families and—at a minimum—to promote two-parent involvement in a child's life. These requirements include such policies as stricter child support enforcement regulations and teen mother living arrangements. The second part of welfare reform focuses on the work requirements designed to assist families in making the transition from welfare to work. This chapter primarily examines the effects of a change in employment and earnings.

In Figure 6.1, these effects on children are mediated by changes in the developmental environment in which the child is raised. That environment has two components: the child's home environment and the environment outside the child's home (primarily day care). The child's home environment comprises the family's economic resources as well as noneconomic aspects,

Figure 6.1. Impact of Leaving Welfare on Children

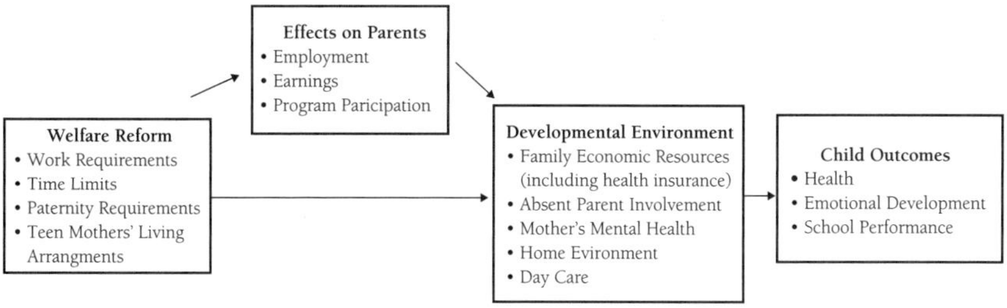

Effects on Parents
- Employment
- Earnings
- Program Pariticipation

Welfare Reform
- Work Requirements
- Time Limits
- Paternity Requirements
- Teen Mothers' Living Arrangments

Developmental Environment
- Family Economic Resources (including health insurance)
- Absent Parent Involvement
- Mother's Mental Health
- Home Evironment
- Day Care

Child Outcomes
- Health
- Emotional Development
- School Performance

including caregiver mental health and involvement with absent parents. Welfare reform may shape a child's developmental environment either directly or indirectly through parental employment and program participation.

Although we do not test the structure of this model, the section on results describes characteristics of leavers and stayers pertaining to key elements of the figure. Moreover, that section presents the outcomes by child-only and single-parent leavers. Although welfare reform generally affects both types of cases, child-only cases are not affected exactly like single-parent cases. For example, caretakers in child-only cases are not subject to work requirements, and there are no time limits for children in child-only cases.

The Role of Child-Only Cases

Because so little is known about child-only cases and the policies concerning these cases in general, we provide a review of the guidelines for their formation. Moreover, we include a description of trends in child-only cases in Georgia specifically.

Unlike a single-parent case, a child-only case is one in which the assistance unit contains no adult. In a single-parent case, that adult typically would be a child's parent (or grandparent). In addition to not wanting to receive assistance, a child's parent might not be included in the assistance unit for any of three reasons: he or she receives Supplemental Security Income (SSI), has legal alien status, or has been removed from the rolls because of failure to comply with program requirements (Office of the Assistant Secretary for Planning and Evaluation, 1999).

Child-only cases always existed under AFDC and TANF, and states have used the program to support kinship caregivers as an alternative to formal involvement with the child welfare system. Although child-only payments are less generous than foster care payments under Title IV-E, the former imposes fewer requirements on caregivers. The family, for example, does not have to relinquish custody of the child or meet the licensing requirements imposed on foster caregivers. Child-only cases also face little if any ongoing supervision by the child welfare system (Office of the

Assistant Secretary for Planning and Evaluation, 1999; U.S. House of Representatives, 1998).

In spite of its emphasis on children, welfare reform does not address child-only cases directly. Nevertheless, the law affects the child-only caseload for several reasons. First, as single-parent cases close, child-only cases may form. This transition could involve the parent's being removed from the assistance unit or the child's moving in with another relative. PRWORA may create some incentive for these transitions. Work requirements and time limits apply only to single-parent cases. As a result, aid received by children does not count against their parents' lifetime limits. Second, the treatment of resident aliens under TANF may influence the size of the child-only caseload. Legal immigrants are specifically banned from receiving TANF for five years. Children born to these families, however, are immediately eligible for TANF (as child-only cases).

The particular way in which welfare reform affects the child-only caseload depends on specific policies that states adopt. Federal law leaves states with enormous flexibility in defining and regulating child-only cases. For example, a state may decide whether a child's (nonrecipient) parent can be present in a household including a child-only case at all.

As a result, the percentage of cases that are child-only varies widely across states. As a percentage of the total caseload, child-only cases varied from around 10 percent (in Alaska and Vermont) to more than 45 percent (in Alabama and Wyoming) of state caseloads. Our figures for Georgia indicate that the state is toward the upper end of this distribution. In January 1997, there were approximately thirty-two thousand child-only cases in Georgia; these cases represented approximately 28 percent of the total active caseload. By October 2000, this figure had risen to 45 percent. The framework for evaluating children can also be used for children in child-only cases, but since time limits and work requirements do not apply, the mediating factors may affect children in child-only cases differently.

Methods

Conducted by Georgia State University, the Georgia leavers' study combines administrative data with an extensive telephone interview involving two hundred or more respondents per month.[2] A family is defined as a leaver if no payment was made to the case for two consecutive months. Interviews occurred roughly six months after the family exited the rolls. The respondents were drawn from cases that closed between November 1998 and January 2001.

The telephone interview covered a wide range of topics. All respondents completed core items concerning demographics, employment, and economic status at the time of the interview, approximately six months after exit from welfare. Respondents also completed a randomly chosen module. The module topics were sources of income and transportation, child care arrangements, mother's mental health and exposure to domestic violence, parenting and home environment, and understanding of welfare reform. Having study participants answer only part of the survey allowed for the inclusion of a wide range of topics in the interview without over-burdening respondents. As a result, the sample sizes vary across the chapter tables. It is important to note that these differences generally were not driven by item nonresponse (that is, by respondents' unwillingness to answer specific questions).

Survey participants were then matched with administrative data from the Georgia Department of Human Resources. These data were used to describe current case status, basic demographic information, relationships among those included in the grant, and any past or current benefit receipt such as Food Stamps or Medicaid.

Approximately 22 percent of the sample consisted of child-only cases. For those cases, interviews were completed with the adult who was responsible for the child when the case was open. (At the time of the interview, that adult might no longer be living with any of the children receiving assistance in the case while open.)

Conducted by the University of Georgia, the Georgia stayers' study consisted of two hundred in-person interviews of individuals still receiving TANF in July 1999. The survey interview overlapped substantially with that used in the leavers study. Approximately 45 percent of the open case sample consisted of child-only cases. This percentage was greater than that for the leavers' sample and reflects the accumulation of child-only cases on the rolls.

In the tables that follow, we compare leavers' and stayers' cases. Although we focus on these differences, we make those comparisons separately for child-only and single-parent cases. Comparisons across panels of the tables will allow readers to compare single-parent and child-only leavers and stayers. The statistical significance associated with any differences across groups was determined by the appropriate statistical test (either a chi-square statistic or a t-test) and refer to leaver-stayer differences.[3]

Results

In this section, we compare outcomes of leavers and stayers comparing the employment and earnings levels of the groups, as well as the earlier identified parental mediating factors and child outcomes.

Basic Demographics. The average age for both leaver and stayer cases was around thirty-five. The two groups differed across a range of other characteristics. For leavers, 61 percent had never been married, compared with 51 percent of those currently receiving benefits. Sixteen percent of stayers were married, compared with only 4 percent of leavers. Education levels also varied between groups, with leavers being more educated. Only 15 percent of stayers reported attending college, compared with 22 percent of leavers. Nearly 60 percent of leavers reported obtaining either a high school diploma or a general equivalency diploma (GED), compared with 51 percent of stayers. Racial differences were also evident. Of leavers, 84 percent were nonwhite, compared with 77 percent of the stayers. Household compositions were relatively similar. Generally, all households had one or two children (68 percent stayers versus 66 percent of leavers). For both groups, approximately 5 percent had more than four children living in the household. Finally, nearly 40 percent of all leavers received benefits for less than one year, compared with only 22 percent of stayers.

Table 6.1 breaks down the demographic differences between single-parent and child-only cases for each of the groups. The most striking within-case-type comparisons are education levels. For single-parent cases, only 28 percent of the leavers had less than a high school education or GED, compared with 41 percent of stayers. Among child-only cases, that difference was even greater. Only 16 percent of caregivers of leavers had less than a high school education or GED, compared with more than half (53 percent) of those caring for children in child-only cases still receiving benefits.

Effects on Parents: Employment and Earnings. There are significant differences in employment. At the time of the interview, 67 percent of leavers were employed, roughly double the rate for those remaining on the rolls (34 percent). Consistent with their higher levels of education, employed leavers had higher earnings. Of those who reported being employed, more than half of all leavers earned more than $800 per month, and 18 percent of those earned more than $1,200 per month. Comparatively, more than 60 percent of stayers earned less than $800 per month, and only 15 percent earned between $800 and $1,200 per month.

Within-case-type comparisons in employment reflect the same trends as the differences between all leavers and all stayers (see Table 6.2). Of single-parent leavers, 67 percent were employed, compared with 39 percent of single-parent stayers. This trend held for child-only leavers and stayers as well (48 percent versus 26 percent). However, there is an interesting trend among earnings (see Table 6.3). Not surprisingly, single-parent stayers' earnings are significantly less than leavers'. Seventy-nine percent of stayers earn less than $800 per month, compared with 33 percent of leavers. However, among child-only cases, half (50 percent) earn less than $800 per month, compared with 26 percent of those who have left. Among stayers, 35 percent earn more than $1,200 per month, compared with 27 percent of leavers.

Developmental Environment. The changes in employment and earnings caused by PWRORA can have an effect on the child's development and environment.

Deprivation Measures. To examine levels of deprivation and need among leavers and stayers, we collected a series of items on food adequacy. The resulting data were mixed. Forty-six percent of leavers stated that they had enough of the types and kinds of food they wanted, compared with a full 74 percent of those remaining on TANF. An additional 41 percent of leavers reported having enough food to eat but not always the kinds they

Table 6.1. Comparison of Single-Parent and Child-Only Groups

		Single-Parent			Child-Only		
		Leavers n=2210	Stayers n=110	p-value	Leavers n=660	Stayers n=91	p-value
Average age		29	29	0.12	45	43	0.00
Marital status	Married	8%	4%	0.03	27%	31%	0.13
	Widowed	2%	0%		12%	10%	
	Divorced	10%	16%		13%	21%	
	Never married	67%	70%		35%	28%	
	Cohabitating	4%	N/A		4%	N/A	
Education	Less than HS	28%	41%	0.00	16%	53%	0.00
	HS or GED	52%	42%		60%	33%	
	Some college	21%	17%		24%	14%	
Race	White	16%	16%	0.02	10%	30%	0.00
	Nonwhite	84%	84%		90%	70%	
Number of kids in the home	1–2 children	61%	72%	0.01	65%	69%	0.03
	3–4 children	30%	24%		28%	24%	
	More than 4	9%	4%		5%	7%	
Months on TANF*	Less than 6 months	21%	12%	0.00	15%	10%	0.00
	6–12 months	21%	15%		15%	9%	
	12–24 months	29%	14%		29%	21%	
	More than 24	29%	59%		41%	60%	

* These results are based on self-reported lifetime use of TANF or AFDC.

would like, compared with 20 percent of stayers. Sixty-seven percent of stayers reported that their child participated in the free or reduced-price lunch program, compared with 87 percent of leavers.

The differences between the subgroups are striking (see Table 6.4). Among single-parent cases, only 13 percent of leavers reported having enough of the types and kinds of food they wanted, compared with 81 percent of stayers. Among child-only cases, 11 percent of leavers reported having enough of the types and kinds of food they wanted, compared with 64 percent of stayers.

Absent Parent Involvement. Despite the efforts of welfare reform to promote the family, respondents in both groups of leavers and stayers overwhelmingly reported little or no involvement with the absent parent (almost exclusively the father). Among leavers, 25 percent had no contact with their absent parent, and 11 percent of stayers reported no contact. Table 6.5 shows these outcomes by case type. Regardless of case type, children still receiving TANF are less likely to see their absent parent (see Table 6.5). Among single-parent cases, 31 percent of leavers never or only

Table 6.2. Leaver and Stayer Employment Groups, by Case Type

	Single-Parent			Child-Only		
	Leavers n=2210	Stayers n=110	p-value	Leavers n=660	Stayers n=91	p-value
Working	67%	39%	0.000	48%	26%	0.000
Retired	1%	0%		10%	12%	
Looking for work	12%	22%		5%	7%	
Disabled	5%	8%		29%	21%	
Housekeeping	8%	13%		6%	21%	
Student	3%	7%		2%	6%	
Other	4%	11%		0%	7%	

once a year visit with their absent parent, compared with 48 percent of stayers. Among child-only cases, 34 percent of leavers never or only once a year visit with their absent parent, compared with more than half (51 percent) of stayers.

Mother's Mental Health. In order to gauge levels of depressive symptoms, respondents were asked to rank a series of questions (for example, "feel tired," "feel nervous," "feel hopeless") from a scale from 1 to 7, with 1 meaning Always and 7 meaning Never. The lower the average number, the stronger the depressive symptoms. Overall, those remaining on TANF showed more depressive symptoms (4.88), compared with those who had left (5.28). While these differences are statistically significant at marginal levels, they are of modest practical magnitude: .20 and .41 standard deviations for single-parent and child-only cases, respectively.

Table 6.3. Leaver and Stayer Earnings, by Case Type

	Single-Parent			Child-Only		
	Leavers n=1106	Stayers n=43	p-value	Leavers n=302	Stayers n=24	p-value
Earnings*						
< $800	33%	79%	0.00	26%	50%	0.00
$800–$1200	50%	16%		47%	15%	
>$1200	17%	5%		27%	35%	
Not working**	31%	61%		55%	74%	
	(n=677)	(n=67)		(n=363)	(n=67)	

* For all groups, this percentage is computed from those individuals who reported being employed at the time of the interview.

** For all groups, respondents who were temporarily laid off, looking for work, retired, students, or housekeepers were coded as not working.

Table 6.4. Leaver and Stayer Deprivation Measures, by Case Type

	Single-Parent			Child-Only		
	Leavers n=1129	Stayers n=110	p-value	Leavers n=280	Stayers n=91	p-value
Had enough of types and kinds of food they wanted	13%	81%	0.00	11%	64%	0.00
Participates in free/reduced price lunch program	86%	96%	0.01	83%	93%	0.01

Home Environment. Three aspects of the home environment that we report here are residential mobility, reported domestic violence, and drug and alcohol abuse. Among all groups, residential mobility was relatively stable. Approximately 70 percent of both leavers and stayers had not moved during the year before they were interviewed. Moreover, only 18 percent of stayers and 14 percent of leavers reported moving once in the past year.

Levels of reported domestic violence and drug and alcohol abuse were also low (see Table 6.6). Among leavers, 6 percent reported being abused by their husband or partner, which is close to the 7 percent reported by stayers. Among leavers, 11 percent reported somebody in the household having a problem with drugs or alcohol, compared with only 5 percent of stayers.

Child Outcomes

Health and Well-Being. Ninety percent of all parents or caregivers in leaver households reported that their children were insured, compared with 97 percent of all children in households still receiving TANF. Of those insured in leaver households, 92 percent were insured by Medicaid or Peachcare, closely

Table 6.5. Leaver and Stayer Absent Parent Involvement, by Case Type

	Single-Parent			Child-Only		
	Leavers n=697	Stayers n=110	p-value	Leavers n=185	Stayers n=91	p-value
Never	25%	11%	0.04	26%	12%	0.01
About once a year	6%	37%		8%	39%	
Several times a year	8%	23%		23%	24%	
1–3 times a month	10%	7%		12%	12%	
About once a week	5%	8%		1%	6%	
Several times a week	10%	15%		14%	7%	

Table 6.6. Home Environment Leavers and Stayers, by Case Type

	Single-Parent			Child-Only		
	Leavers n=2210	Stayers n=110	p-value	Leavers n=660	Stayers n=91	p-value
Average depression score	5.44	5.19	0.09	5.13	4.63	0.04
One move or more	25% n=510	23% n=110	0.56	38% n=147	24% n=91	0.16
Reported domestic violence	6%	9%	0.31	3%	4%	0.27
Reported problem with drugs or alcohol	10%	5%	0.11	11%	5%	0.09

resembling the percentage of children in households still receiving TANF (94 percent). Among leaver households, 78 percent of parents or caregivers reported that the children were generally in excellent or very good health, compared with 87 percent of those still receiving TANF. Finally, 5 percent of parents or caregivers in leaver households reported caring for a disabled child, compared with 8 percent of respondents in households still receiving aid.

Comparing case type, the results are similar except for type of insurance for child-only cases (see Table 6.7). Leavers are less likely than stayers to use Medicaid or Peachcare (88 percent versus 98 percent) and are more likely to use employer-provided insurance (8 percent versus 2 percent).

Child Care Arrangements. Table 6.8 describes child care arrangements among study children. (Because parents can identify multiple sources of care, each column may not total 100 percent.) The table reveals significant differences between child-only and single-parent cases and between leavers and stayers. Among leavers, children in child-only cases are cared for most commonly by a nonrelative sitter (44 percent) or are enrolled in a Head Start center (33 percent). Like child-only cases, the largest portion of children in closed single-parent cases are cared for by a nonrelative sitter (47 percent), followed by a Head Start program (42 percent). Among stayers, the choice of child care arrangements is more evenly distributed among child care options.

Conclusion

Our tabulations provide a variety of interesting insights into the well-being of children leaving welfare in Georgia. Like many other studies, we find that families leaving welfare have joined the ranks of the working poor. They are working but at low wages. Most remain off the welfare rolls. These patterns generally apply to both child-only and single-parent leavers. We compared our findings for leavers with a small sample of stayers. To the extent that

Table 6.7. Leavers' and Stayers' Child Health, by Case Type

	Single-Parent			Child-Only		
	Leavers n=1144	Stayers n=110	p-value	Leavers n=586	Stayers n=91	p-value
Child insured	89%	96%	0.00	91%	97%	0.01
Type of insurance Medicaid/						
Peachcare	93%	96%	0.51	88%	98%	0.00
Employer provided	5%	3%		8%	2%	
Self-provided	2%	1%		4%	0%	
Reported disabled	6%	7%	0.71	4%	7%	0.38
General health good/excellent	80%	86%	0.09	73%	87%	0.00

Table 6.8. Leavers' and Stayers' Child Care Arrangements, by Case Type

	Single-Parent			Child-Only		
	Leavers n=792	Stayers n=80	p-value	Leavers n=285	Stayers n=32	p-value
Nonrelative sitter	47%	10%	0.03	44%	13%	0.03
Care in relative homes	5%	20%		0%	11%	
Care in nonrelative homes	3%	13%		0%	12%	
Head start center	42%	23%		33%	11%	
PreK/nursery program	5%	33%		0%	33%	
Child stays alone	4%	1%		0%	0%	

they provide a sense of how leavers fared while on the rolls, these figures provide a rough sense of how leaving has affected the families exiting the rolls. Comparisons with stayers, for example, indicate that leavers are more likely to be working. This comparison is consistent with the claim that leaving welfare increases employment, but the between-group difference is likely an overestimate of that effect. Leavers differ from stayers in many ways and so may have been working more even while on welfare. For example, leavers are better educated and have spent less time on welfare. Nonetheless, it seems likely that leavers have increased their employment.

In general, leavers are faring better than stayers economically, and this difference extends to other dimensions of well-being, such as mental health. Levels of depression, for example, are higher among stayers. Without pre-exit data, however, one cannot conclude that leaving welfare improves mental health. Depression may be a barrier to leaving welfare, and in that case, the observed differences existed even while the leavers were on the rolls.

Within the state of Georgia, we were able to confirm our initial supposition: dramatic differences were apparent between child-only and single-parent leavers. Child-only leavers generally had spent less time on welfare and were somewhat better educated. However, the caregivers in those cases were less likely to be employed at the time of the interview and more likely to identify themselves as disabled. Single-parent leavers reported their children were in better health than did child-only leavers. Access to insurance among children was generally good, although very few children had access to insurance through their parents' employment.

These findings provide useful insight into the well-being of children under welfare reform and into diversity among leavers. At least as reported by their caregivers, children are in good health, and only a small minority lack access to health insurance. Insurance coverage is lower among both groups of leavers. In addition, parent reports of their children's health is lower as well.

Since child-only laws vary by state, these conclusions are not generalizable to other states. However, these results do beg an interesting question that should be addressed: How do children in child-only cases fare in states that have less stringent child-only regulations? In Georgia, if a mother simply leaves TANF (not for SSI) in order for the child to continue to receive assistance, the child must move in with a specified relative. Other states do not require the child to move away from his or her mother. These circumstances would create a different picture of children living in child-only cases.

These findings are limited by the structure of our study. A fuller assessment of child well-being would require data from multiple informants, including teachers and, in the case of young children, observational data. Perhaps most important is our inability to describe the effect of leaving welfare. Comparisons with stayers provide only an estimate, and those comparisons are fairly imprecise (due to the small size of the stayers' sample).

Nonetheless, these findings are among the very few to consider the status of child-only leavers (or child-only stayers, for that matter). This information is particularly useful in the light of their continued growth as a proportion of the overall caseload. The differences between child-only and single-parent stayers highlight further shifts in the welfare caseload, of which policymakers should be cognizant as they craft policies about who remains on the rolls.

Notes

1. The literature underlying Figure 6.1 is reviewed in Rickman (2001).
2. The response rate for the telephone survey averaged 65 percent and was the same for both single-parent and child-only cases.
3. Supplemental tabulations of statistical significance for comparisons of single-parent and child-only cases are available from the first author.

References

Georgia Department of Human Resources. *Economic Support Services Manual*. Atlanta: Department of Human Resources, 1999.

Lewin Group. "Understanding the AFDC/TANF Child-Only Caseload: Policies, Composition, and Characteristics in Three States." [aspe.hhs.gov/hsp/child-only-caseload00/index.htm]. 2000.

Murray, C. "What to Do About Welfare." In J. A. Hird and M. Reese (eds.), *Controversies in American Public Policy*. New York: Russell Sage Foundation, 1999.

Office of the Assistant Secretary for Planning and Evaluation. "Questions Concerning Child-Only Cases." [aspe.hhs.gov/hsp/FAQ-Child-Only99/childonlyfaq.htm]. 1999.

Rickman, D. K. "The Effects of Leaving TANF on Children: A Comparison of Single-Parent Leavers and Child-Only Cases." Working paper, Georgia State University, 2001.

U.S. House of Representatives. Committee on Ways and Means. *Overview of Entitlement Programs: 1998 Green Book*. Washington, D.C.: U.S. Government Printing Office, 1998.

DANA K. RICKMAN *is a graduate student in the Department of Political Science and Research Associate at the Applied Research Center at Georgia State University.*

E. MICHAEL FOSTER *is associate professor of health policy and administration at The Pennsylvania State University.*

This chapter uses cluster analysis to distinguish three groups of leavers of Temporary Assistance to Needy Families in terms of their self-reported well-being after exit, verifies these clusters, and then uses classification tree analysis to isolate some of the factors that may be responsible for these differences in post-exit outcomes.

7

Acknowledging Different Needs: Developing a Taxonomy of Welfare Leavers

George Julnes, Kentaro Hayashi, Steven Anderson

Inspired by a sense that welfare entitlements were encouraging a culture of dependency, Congress passed the Personal Responsibility and Work Opportunity Reconciliation Act of 1996 (PRWORA), replacing the Aid to Families with Dependent Children (AFDC) program with the Temporary Assistance to Needy Families (TANF) programs. Although the decreasing TANF caseloads across the nation provide some evidence of the success of this round of welfare reform, there is still an important role for evaluators to play in understanding the outcomes of the current policies and guiding the next round of reform.

In order to be of most use, evaluators need to address the information needs of policymakers. We argue that much of the research on welfare reform is limited to a few traditional approaches and that there is value to incorporating multiple perspectives to inform the welfare reform dialogue. We present in this chapter research that focuses on the well-being of people

The analyses described in this chapter were conducted on the basis of a cooperative agreement with the Illinois Department of Human Services and the U.S. Department of Health and Human Services (grant 98ASPEC298A). The opinions and conclusions expressed here, however, are solely the authors' and should not be interpreted as reflecting the opinions and policies of the federal government or the state of Illinois.

We express our appreciation to Motoya Machida for providing technical support for Splus functions.

who left welfare in Illinois (referred to as TANF leavers) and uses their assessments of their well-being to identify distinct groups of those leavers. That is, we use the leavers' post-TANF well-being outcomes to create a taxonomy of leavers—a categorization of leavers into groups based on whether they are succeeding after leaving welfare, struggling, or somewhere in the middle. After validating the meaning of our derived categories, or clusters, of leavers, we then examine the factors that seem most important in distinguishing between those who succeed after leaving welfare and those who do not. These findings are relevant for potential policy changes that might better meet the needs of those leaving welfare.

Incorporating Multiple Perspectives to Inform Welfare Policy

Now that the TANF programs have been in place for five years, research is starting to provide answers to a variety of questions, such as the percentage of TANF leavers who remain employed for twelve months after exit, the factors that predict employment after exit, and reasons that some eligible leavers are not participating in the Medicaid and Food Stamps programs. And yet as McClintock and Lowe point out in Chapter Two of this volume, questions remain. Some questions will likely never be answered, but we may also be limiting our ability to answer important questions by limiting the methods used to conduct research on welfare reform. For example, much of the research in this area is one of two types: based on simple cross-tabulations that show results over time or across region, or more complex efforts to use something like regression analysis to isolate the influences of specific factors on identified outcome fields.

Although each of these approaches has strengths, there are alternatives that should also be considered in particular contexts. Indeed, consistent with Cook's (1985) critical multiplism framework, providing the necessary information generally requires employing multiple perspectives.

Multiple Sources of Data and Multiple Analyses. The first points to make about incorporating multiple perspectives relate to the general goals of this volume. First, both survey and administrative data were used—survey data to represent the perspectives of the TANF leavers and administrative data to validate the results of cluster analysis. Second, cluster analysis was used to create a taxonomy of TANF leavers. Unlike the more typical R-analyses that yield relationships among variables, cluster analysis is a form of Q-analysis that solves for relationships among individuals (Rummel, 1970).

Balancing Valued Outcomes. One complicating factor in providing relevant information is that we almost always confront conflicting values in evaluation. Berlin (1990) highlighted the conflict between liberty and equality when thinking about public policy ("total liberty for wolves is death to the lambs," p. 297). Similarly, Okun (1975) emphasized the conflict between—and thus the need to balance—the pursuit of equality and efficiency in public policy. If an evaluation were to provide information on only one of these values, it would feel incomplete and be seen as less relevant.

In the context of welfare policy, there is a strong distinction between those whose research focuses on the efficiency implications of particular policies (Robins, Michalopoulos, and Pan, 2001) and those who are more interested in the effect of welfare reform on the health and dignity of the more disadvantaged in society (Mink, 1998). For the former, the outcomes studied include the administrative goals of increasing the employment effort of those who leave welfare and decreasing their recidivism to TANF cash assistance (see Chapters Four and Five in this volume). For the latter, a major concern is the well-being of those who have left TANF (Green, 2000; Schram, 1995). In that much of the research on welfare reform has emphasized administrative efficiency (see Chapter Two, this volume), this chapter provides balance by studying the well-being of former TANF clients. Although there are several ways to measure well-being (Ringen, 1997), we will work from the perspectives of the former clients, measuring such things as the TANF leavers' self-reported hardships and their satisfaction after leaving welfare.

Recognizing Different Types of Leavers. A second complicating factor for evaluations is that results are often reported in the aggregate (for example, "Seventy-five percent of leavers are employed six months after exit"), but we are just as often concerned about the outcomes that particular groups experience. Although much of the recent research on welfare reform emphasizes the aggregate perspective, it is worth reviewing welfare studies that did emphasize individual differences among welfare leavers. For example, welfare spell lengths (the number of months or years that someone is continuously receiving welfare payments) are highly variable and have links with several outcomes of interest. This has led some analysts to classify recipients according to length of spell (Duncan, 1984; Bane and Ellwood, 1994). The rationale for this distinction is that the long spells of a subset of welfare recipients, when coupled with poor education and limited job skills, point to a particular public policy concern (Jencks, 1992). Others have paid particular attention to another group of leavers: welfare recipients who leave cash assistance but then recidivate (Edin and Lein, 1997; Harris, 1996). More recently, Moffitt and Roff (2000) found that employment and other outcomes differed according to educational level, health status, prior dependence on welfare, and whether they were sanctioned from TANF.

Notice that in each of the studies that sought to disaggregate their findings, the leavers are distinguished on variables that are believed or known to be important, such as welfare spell length, education, or psychological deficits. An alternative approach to disaggregation is to proceed inductively and allow the data to determine who is grouped together. In this approach, referred to as a taxonomy (in contrast to typologies; see Bailey, 1994), having similar values on a number of variables leads to classification in the same group. For example, some studies have shown that different subsets of TANF leavers experience a widely differing array of employment barriers, including both psychological and human capital deficits (Danziger and others, 2000; Danziger, Kalil, and Anderson, 1998; Jayakody, Danziger, and Pollack, 2000; Zedlewski, 1999). For our purposes, it is particularly useful to develop categories based on the leavers' views of how they have fared after leaving welfare. Using cluster analysis, the result is a taxonomy that groups leavers according to their post-TANF well-being. The rationale for developing this taxonomy is that identifying groups of TANF leavers according to their post-TANF outcomes is important if we are to tailor welfare policies to meet the particular needs of different subpopulations.

Methodology

The analyses in this chapter are based on a study of persons who left TANF during the early months of program implementation in Illinois. The study was one of fourteen studies from a project sponsored by the Office of the Assistant Secretary for Program Evaluation (ASPE) with the U.S. Department of Health and Human Services (DHHS). It used both administrative records and survey data to analyze economic well-being and other outcome measures for TANF leavers. The study was conducted by a team of researchers from the University of Illinois at Springfield and the University of Illinois at Urbana/Champaign (Julnes and others, 2000), with the assistance of both funding and technical support from the Illinois Department of Human Services (IDHS). The study used administrative and survey data to conduct and interpret cluster analysis and classification tree.

Research Population and Sample. The population being studied with administrative data consisted of all TANF cases in Illinois that closed at least once between July 1997 and December 1998. This resulted in a population of 137,330 cases, the large majority being single-parent cases headed by women. In contrast, the survey involved 514 respondents out of a pool of 1,001 cases, or a 51 percent response rate. The survey sample left TANF in December 1998, which corresponded to the final administrative data cohort for the project. This response rate reflected the difficulty in locating TANF leavers rather than high refusal rates. Comparisons of respondents and nonrespondents using the administrative data files suggested that the sample well represented the leaver population in most key respects.

Data. The administrative data used for this analysis are derived primarily from the IDHS Client Database (CDB), with wage data from the Illinois Department of Employment Security (IDES) quarterly wage files.[1] Variables on these administrative files include dates of program coverage (on, for example, TANF, Food Stamps, and Medicaid), reasons for TANF case closure, and demographic information (birthdates of people on the case, education of adult on the case, and marital status of the adult on the case).

Survey content, guided by ASPE-sponsored dialogues with other state researchers, focused on the experiences of TANF leavers when leaving TANF and in the months immediately after TANF exit. Although a wide array of topics was included, we emphasized employment experiences and the well-being of clients. The survey contained questions about leaver circumstances at the time of TANF exit and interview six to eight months later. In addition, selected questions asked about the experiences of leavers before the TANF exit. Including such questioning for selected time periods allowed for limited analyses across time even though the survey was administered at a single point in time. The average length of the interview was just over thirty minutes.

Analyses. As an overview of the analyses used, cluster analysis was employed to create groupings of leavers. The meaning of these groupings was validated by examining group differences on other variables, and then classification tree analysis was used to interpret the important differences between those who succeed after leaving TANF and those who do not.

Cluster Analysis. The first step was to create a taxonomy of leavers based on their self-reported well-being. Cluster analysis was selected for this task because of its familiarity to many researchers and its minimal assumptions that make it rather robust across contexts (Aldenderfer and Blashfield, 1984; Julnes, 1999). The basic idea of this family of methods is to create groupings that minimize within-group distances relative to between-group distances. Although the procedure is fairly robust relative to assumptions, one potential difficulty is that it will assign people to categories whether or not such categories are real (Bailey, 1994). Another challenge is that various method choices (such as the survey questions to include) can markedly affect the clusters that result. Three categories of questions were used as indicators of well-being: post-TANF hardships experienced, current satisfaction with aspects of life, and assessment of whether aspects of life are better after exit.

Validation. Recognizing the tendency of cluster analysis to create categories whether or not they represent real differences, we sought to validate the meaningfulness of the categories derived by a sequential process that compares the resultant groups on other variables (for a more comprehensive approach to sequential validation, see Humphreys and Rosenheck, 1995). Of particular interest is using information from other data sources, in this case the administrative data. To the extent that these other variables provide expected relationships with the clusters, the interpretation of these clusters is supported.

Interpretation: Classification Tree Analysis. Once the clusters were identified and validated with additional variables, we addressed the question of what factors might be responsible for some TANF clients succeeding after exit and others not. Variants of regression analysis would provide coefficients that predicted group membership, but there is an alternative that has several advantages over the specification of abstract relationships between variables that is the hallmark of regression analysis: classification tree analysis.

The theory behind tree-based models (with either continuous or categorical dependent variables) was introduced by Breiman, Friedman, Olshen, and Stone (1984). The models provide an alternative exploratory analysis to linear models for regression problems and linear logistic models for classification problems (Clark and Pregibon, 1993). Results of tree-based analyses might seem similar to those generated by hierarchical cluster analysis (Julnes, 1999), but there are fundamental differences, including the distinction made in tree-based analyses between response variables and predictor variables, a distinction that cluster analysis does not make.

As Clark and Pregibon (1993) point out, several features give tree-based models advantages over traditional linear models:

Tree-based models can be easier to interpret when the set of predictors contains a mixture of numeric and categorical variables.

Tree-based models have the advantage of being invariant to monotone reexpressions of predictor variables.

Missing values are handled particularly well by tree-based models.

Tree-based models are particularly flexible in depicting complex interactions (referred to as nonadditive behaviors), where, for example, some predictor variables are more important for some subgroups than others.

This last advantage deserves additional comment. First, classification tree analysis begins by classifying individuals with the goal of trying to mirror the distribution in the outcome variable. After dividing the total set of cases into two groups, classification tree analysis looks for variables that then subdivide these two groups into two more subgroups each. In contrast to regression analysis, this next step need not use the same variable to subdivide the first two groups into four. It is often the case, as we show, that one subgroup is best divided by one variable, with the other subgroup divided by another variable.

These advantages have led to increasing use of tree-based models, particularly since SPlus (MathSoft, 1998) functions became available, but the tree-based models are still unfamiliar statistical techniques for many in the program evaluation community. In addition to using this technique to sharpen our understanding of the dynamics of post-TANF outcomes, an additional goal of this chapter is to introduce tree-based models and their rich possibilities for use in evaluation.

Results

Cluster analysis led to separating the former TANF clients in the survey sample (506 with complete data) into three groups. Judging from the descriptive statistics for the three groups on three sets of variables (hardships after leaving TANF; satisfaction with aspects of life after leaving TANF; and assessment of whether life is better, the same, or worse), we named the three groups as the success group (comprising 97 leavers), the intermediate group (211 leavers), and the struggle group (198 leavers; see Table 7.1).

To highlight some of the differences among groups, note that whereas only 6 percent of those in the success group indicated that they had to skip meals for

Table 7.1. Cluster Description and Validation: Variable Means by Cluster

Variables Used in Clustering	Clusters of Leavers in Terms of Well-Being		
	Success	Intermediate	Struggle
Hardships after exit[a]			
Got behind in rent	0.155 (0.363)	0.174 (0.380)	0.702 (0.459)
Had to move out	0.010 (0.102)	0.027 (0.164)	0.278 (0.449)
No medical care	0.072 (0.260)	0.187 (0.391)	0.535 (0.500)
Skipped meals	0.062 (0.242)	0.091 (0.289)	0.551 (0.499)
No money for food	0.206 (0.407)	0.237 (0.426)	0.783 (0.413)
Current satisfaction[b]			
Overall	1.577 (0.556)	1.688 (0.564)	2.731 (0.871)
Financial condition	1.773 (0.771)	2.097 (0.725)	3.465 (0.717)
Housing conditions	1.598 (0.837)	1.739 (0.832)	2.540 (1.040)
Personal health	1.381 (0.603)	1.608 (0.757)	2.096 (0.949)
Health care	1.333 (0.592)	1.912 (0.948)	2.702 (1.102)
Better after exit[c]			
Money available	0.866 (0.342)	0.680 (0.467)	0.131 (0.339)
Provide for family	0.959 (0.200)	0.644 (0.480)	0.131 (0.339)
Med. care for children	0.938 (0.242)	0.050 (0.219)	0.071 (0.257)
Med. care for self	0.907 (0.292)	0.032 (0.176)	0.086 (0.281)
Your health	0.701 (0.460)	0.242 (0.429)	0.091 (0.288)
Housing	0.722 (0.451)	0.374 (0.485)	0.121 (0.327)
Self-esteem	0.907 (0.292)	0.721 (0.449)	0.258 (0.438)
Child's view of parent	0.639 (0.483)	0.507 (0.501)	0.293 (0.456)
Overall assessment	0.918 (0.277)	0.749 (0.435)	0.197 (0.399)
Validation with additional variables			
Quarterly wages after exit	$2267 (2226)	$1525 (2039)	$1045 (1514)
Years on welfare	4.066 (4.309)	5.205 (5.064)	5.918 (5.726)
Monthly household income	$1821(2079)	$1297 (1149)	$850 (962)
Cluster sizes	N = 97	N = 211	N = 198

Note: Standard deviations are in parentheses.
[a]Coded as 1 for "experienced hardship" and 0 otherwise.
[b]Coded as 1 for very satisfied, 2 for somewhat satisfied, 3 for somewhat dissatisfied, and 4 for very dissatisfied.
[c]Coded as 1 for "better after exit" and 0 otherwise.

lack of money sometime in the six months after leaving TANF, over half of those in the struggle group had indicated having experienced this hardship. For this hardship of skipping meals, those in the intermediate group were quite close to the success group. This pattern was seen for many of the variables used to generate the three clusters (see also the variables for overall current satisfaction and overall assessment of life being better after exit). A significant exception to this pattern was whether medical care, for either the leavers or their children, was better or worse after leaving TANF. As seen in Table 7.1, whereas over 90 percent of those in the success group viewed medical care for their children as better than when they were on TANF, almost none (5 percent; similar to the 2.6 percent for the struggle cluster) of those in the intermediate cluster indicated that this medical care was now better. Less stark but still substantial were the differences between the success cluster and the intermediate cluster on ratings of leaver's health (70 percent indicating better since exit versus 24 percent) and housing (72 percent indicating better since exit versus 37 percent).

Validation. In order to make sure that these groupings are not just artifacts of chance or some response set, we related these clusters to other variables and found, for example, that, as expected and reported in Table 7.1, the success group reported a higher monthly household income ($1,821) than the other two groups (respectively, $1,297 and $850 for the intermediate and the struggling groups). Other variables, also reported in Table 7.1, validated the meaningfulness of the clusters. For example, the struggle group had been on TANF cash assistance longer prior to this latest exit than the other two groups (5.9 years versus 5.2 and 4.1 years for the success categories). Even more telling, information from a different data source confirmed the expected relationships, with the IDES unemployment wage data showing the highest average quarterly earnings in the quarter after exit for the success group ($2,267), with the struggle group having the lowest average salaries ($1,045, with $1,525 for the intermediate group).

Interpretation. As for attempting interpretations of the factors responsible for these between-group differences, the categorical variable cluster, which consists of the assignment of individuals into one of the three groups, served as the response variable for our classification tree. The following predictors were employed, based partly on previous research and partly on subsequent examination of the set of variables:

- Monthly household income.
- Region: Chicago–Cook County versus the rest of the state
- Child care needs (5-point scale based on four questions about difficulties arranging child care).
- Hourly wages.
- Informal social support, a scale based on five questions like, "How often do you have someone you can count on to lend you some money if you really needed it?" With each answer scored from 1 to 6, this five-question scale can range from 5 for always having the five types of support to 30 for never having any of these supports.
- Age at TANF exit (December 1998).
- Recidivism.
- Non-Medicaid health insurance.
- Work experience (categorical variable indicating experience, for example, as a manager or service worker, or no experience).

- High school diploma (or more).
- Case closed for noncooperation (for example, the client failed to show up for a meeting or to report earnings).
- Work barriers.
- Number of years on welfare (self-reported total years and months as an adult).

The total number of subjects with complete data for this analysis was 402. Particularly with sample sizes as large as this, a critical question for this type of analysis is the number of groupings that are to be reported. Although there are formulas that are sometimes used to make this determination using deviation scores and the cost-complexity parameters, this decision often benefits from judgment. Based on the value we placed on parsimony, we pruned the tree and obtained a solution with seven terminal nodes (with terminal nodes represented as rectangles in Figure 7.1).

First Split: Child Care Needs. Consistent with the results for cluster analysis, 17 percent of the subjects are in the success group, and 40 percent of the subjects are in the struggle group, with the remainder in the intermediate group. As seen in Figure 7.1, the first split was made based on whether child care needs were being met (the variable is coded so that low numbers indicate few needs, with the criterion value of 1.5 or lower indicating very few needs). With this split, 157 subjects belonged to the group in which child care needs

Figure 7.1. Classification Tree Analysis: Factors Associated with Clusters

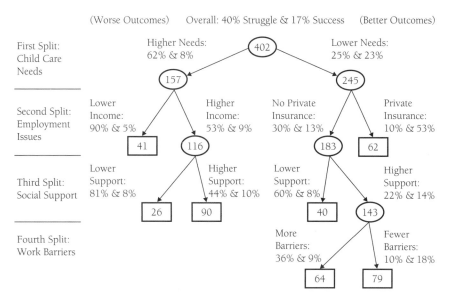

Note: Shown are the percentages of each group in the struggle and success clusters.

are high, and 245 subjects belonged to the group with low child care needs. This division addresses many of the distinctions among the clusters: only 8 percent of those reporting high child care needs were in the success group, and 62 percent of those reporting such needs were in the struggle group. In comparison, of 245 former TANF clients reporting low child care needs, the success group (23 percent) and the struggle group (25 percent) were almost evenly split.

Second Split: Employment Issues. Moving to the next level of the classification tree, and looking first at the left side with the 157 respondents who reported high child care needs, we see that the next split criterion was whether monthly household income was above $438.50. When the monthly household income was below $438.50 (41 people), only 5 percent belonged to the success group and 90 percent to the struggle group, indicating the worst outcome on this classification tree. Even when the monthly household income was above $438.50 (116 people), outcomes were still poor, with 9 percent in the success group and 53 percent in the struggle group. Moving to the right side of the tree, with the 245 people who reported low child care needs, the next split criterion was whether they had non-Medicaid health insurance (listed as private health insurance). This split is included under the loose label of employment in that it is likely that coverage by health insurance other than Medicaid generally reflects having quality employment that offers such benefits. Accordingly, those having non-Medicaid health insurance (62 people) were particularly likely, at 53 percent, to be in the success cluster; only 10 percent in the struggle cluster had non-Medicaid insurance. This was the only terminal node with the majority of people in the success category. On the other hand, the group without non-Medicaid health insurance (183 people) had 13 percent in the success cluster and 30 percent in the struggle cluster.

Third Split: Social Support. The group with monthly household income above $438.50 was split one more time by whether the leaver had informal social support (22.5 and higher on a scale that ranges from 5 to 30 indicates only minimal social support). For the 90 respondents with at least some social support (scores below the criterion of 22.5), 10 percent were in the success cluster and 44 percent in the struggle cluster. For the 26 people without even this minimal degree of social support, the profile was worse. Only 8 percent were in the success cluster, and 81 percent were in the struggle cluster. On the right side of the figure, the group of 183 leavers without non-Medicaid health insurance went through another split by whether they had social support (coded here by the criterion of 19.5, with higher numbers indicating less support). The group without social support (40 people) had only 8 percent in the success category and 60 percent in the struggle category. The group with social support (143 people) offers a somewhat better profile: only 14 percent in the success cluster but also only 22 percent in the struggle cluster.

Fourth Split: Work Barriers. The latter group split one more time, by whether work barriers were a problem. The group reporting more work barriers (64 people) had 9 percent in the success group and 36 percent in the struggle group, and the group reporting fewer work barriers (79 people) had 18 percent in the success group and 10 percent in the struggle group.

Conclusion

The intent of this chapter was to identify groups of TANF leavers in terms of their self-reported well-being outcomes. The hope of this effort was that by distinguishing those who succeed after leaving TANF from others who struggle to differing degrees, we would be in a better position to inform the policy debates on welfare reform regarding varying program interventions. We showed, for example, that there is a large group of TANF leavers (211 of 506, or just over 40 percent) who are similar to the most successful leavers in terms of their overall satisfaction with life after TANF, with the distinct exception of medical care. It would seem that whereas those in the success group are employed in jobs with medical insurance as a benefit, those in the intermediate cluster are employed without such benefits. This highlights medical coverage as a particular need of this large group of leavers, and one that if not addressed might result in higher-than-necessary recidivism rates among this group. Thus, one policy implication of this study is that in addition to the most and the least successful of TANF leavers, there are many leavers who are marginally successful and who could be well served with only a few additional public supports.

The classification tree analysis added to this awareness about medical coverage, but the tree's first point was to suggest that differences among the success, intermediate, and struggle clusters could be accounted for well by an understanding of the self-reported child care needs of the former TANF clients. Partly in response to this study, Illinois is devoting considerable resources to child care subsidies, to the extent that over 200,000 children are now receiving this subsidy. That the group without child care needs could be further divided in terms of non-Medicaid medical insurance reinforced the importance of medical coverage for the working poor. Various solutions have been suggested for this prevalent need among TANF leavers (including broader but less complete medical coverage for the poor), and further research may be able to clarify which of the alternatives address the needs of different leavers.

The final policy point from the classification tree analysis was the importance of social support (measured by leavers indicating the degree to which they have friends or relatives who can lend them money, provide transportation, and watch their children) for distinguishing leavers in terms of after-TANF well-being. These findings reinforce the results of other analyses of these data in indicating that there is a subgroup of leavers who are socially isolated and not receiving the public supports to which they are entitled (see Chapter Four, this volume). Although public policy need not view social isolation as a public need, policies can be developed that are sensitive to the needs of such leavers.

Having summarized some substantive conclusions of this research, we close by reiterating some of the comments made previously about how this study used multiple perspectives in developing its conclusions. First, we incorporated multiple data sources and multiple levels of aggregation in the analyses. Second, we made use of methods (cluster analysis as a Q-analysis and classification tree analysis; see Julnes, 1999, and Breiman, Friedman, Olshen, and Stone, 1984) and values (leaver well-being) often neglected in welfare research. The intent is that this incorporation of multiple perspectives will provide a richer view of the outcomes experienced by those who leave TANF, a view that will be relevant to a broader array of stakeholders and so more central to policy debates ahead.

Note

1. The data collection and processing are described in more detail in the final report for the project (Julnes and others, 2000). This report and the survey are available at ipa.uis.edu/published_rpts.htm.

References

Aldenderfer, M. E., and Blashfield, R. K. *Cluster Analysis.* Thousand Oaks, Calif.: Sage, 1984.

Bailey, K. D. *Typologies and Taxonomies: An Introduction to Classification Techniques.* Thousand Oaks, Calif.: Sage, 1994.

Bane, M. J., and Ellwood, D. T. *Welfare Realities: From Rhetoric to Reform.* Cambridge, Mass.: Harvard University Press, 1994.

Berlin, I. *The Crooked Timber of Humanity: Chapters in the History of Ideas.* (H. Hardy, ed.) Princeton, N.J.: Princeton University Press, 1990.

Breiman, L., Friedman, J. H., Olshen, R. A., and Stone, C. J. *Classification and Regression Trees.* Belmont, Calif.: Wadsworth, 1984.

Clark, L. A., and Pregibon, D. "Tree-Based Models." In J. M. Chambers and T. J. Hastie (eds.), *Statistical Models in S.* New York: Chapman and Hall, 1993.

Cook, T. D. "Postpositivist Critical Multiplism." In L. Shotland and M. M. Mark (eds.), *Social Science and Social Policy.* Thousand Oaks, Calif.: Sage, 1985.

Danziger, S. K., Kalil, A., and Anderson, N. J. "Human Capital, Health and Mental Health of Welfare Recipients: Co-Occurrence and Correlates." *Journal of Social Issues,* 1998, *54,* 637–656.

Danziger, S. K., and others. "Barriers to the Employment of Welfare Recipients." In R. Cherry and W. M. Rodgers (eds.), *Prosperity for All? The Economic Boom and African Americans.* New York: Russell Sage Foundation, 2000.

Duncan, G. T. *Years of Poverty, Years of Plenty.* Ann Arbor: Institute for Social Research, University of Michigan, 1984.

Edin, K., and Lein, L. *Making Ends Meet.* New York: Russell Sage Foundation, 1997.

Green, J. "Tough Sanctions, Tough Luck." *American Prospect,* 2000, *11,* 38.

Harris, K. M. "Life After Welfare: Women, Work, and Repeat Dependency." *American Sociological Review,* 1996, *61,* 407–426.

Humphreys, K., and Rosenheck, R. "Sequential Validation of Cluster Analytic Subtypes of Homeless Veterans." *American Journal of Community Psychology,* 1995, *23,* 75–98.

Jayakody, R., Danziger, S. H., and Pollack, H. "Welfare Reform, Substance Use, and Mental Health." *Journal of Health Politics, Policy, and Law,* 2000, *25,* 623–651.

Jencks, C. *Rethinking Social Policy: Race, Poverty, and the Underclass.* Cambridge, Mass.: Harvard University Press, 1992.

Julnes, G. "Principal Component Analysis, Factor Analysis, and Cluster Analysis." In G. J. Miller and M. L. Whicker (eds.), *Handbook of Data Analysis and Quantitative Methods in Public Administration.* New York: Marcel Dekker, 1999.

Julnes, G., and others. *Illinois Study of Former TANF Clients, Final Report.* Champaign: University of Illinois for the Illinois Department of Human Services, Aug. 2000.

Mark, M. M., Henry, G. T., and Julnes, G. *Evaluation: An Integrated Framework for Understanding, Guiding, and Improving Policies and Programs.* San Francisco: Jossey-Bass, 2000.

MathSoft. *S-Plus 5 for UNIX: Guide to Statistics.* Seattle, Wash.: MathSoft, 1998.

Mink, G. *Welfare's End.* Ithaca, N.Y.: Cornell University Press, 1998.

Moffitt, R., and Roff, J. *The Diversity of Welfare Leavers. Welfare, Children, and Families: A Three City Study.* Baltimore, Md.: John Hopkins University, 2000.

Okun, A. M. *Equality and Efficiency: The Big Tradeoff.* Washington, D.C.: Brookings Institution, 1975.

Ringen, S. *Citizens, Families, and Reform.* New York: Oxford University Press, 1997.

Robins, P. K., Michalopoulos, C., and Pan, E. "Financial Incentives and Welfare Reform in the United States." *Journal of Policy Analysis and Management,* 2001, 20, 129–149.

Rummel, R. J. *Applied Factor Analysis.* Evanston, Ill.: Northwestern University Press, 1970.

Schram, S. F. *Words of Welfare: The Poverty of Social Science and the Social Science of Poverty.* Minneapolis: University of Minnesota Press, 1995.

Zedlewski, S. R. *Work Activity and Obstacles to Work Among TANF Recipients: Assessing the New Federalism.* Washington, D.C.: Urban Institute, 1999.

GEORGE JULNES is assistant professor of psychology with the Research and Evaluation Methodology Program and director of the Center for Policy and Program Evaluation at Utah State University.

KENTARO HAYASHI is assistant professor of psychology with the Research and Evaluation Methodology Program and senior researcher in the Center for Policy and Program Evaluation at Utah State University.

STEVE ANDERSON is assistant professor at the School of Social Work, University of Illinois at Urbana-Champaign

8

The expansion of income and service supports to reinforce work efforts has been an important component of welfare reform. This chapter examines support service use patterns by leavers of Temporary Assistance to Needy Families, as well as reasons for nonuse of services.

Support Service Use Patterns by Early TANF Leavers

Steven G. Anderson, Anthony P. Halter, Richard Schuldt

The need to improve support services for low-wage workers has been a common theme in welfare reform debates (Danziger, 1999). Even before the Personal Responsibility and Work Opportunity Reconciliation Act (PRWORA) was passed in 1996, the prior decade had witnessed substantial expansions of Medicaid, child care services, and the earned income tax credit (EITC). PRWORA has provided states with fiscal and administrative flexibility to redesign support service systems for TANF leavers. Nonetheless, declining Medicaid and Food Stamp caseloads since PRWORA raise questions about why services sometimes are not used. In addition, variations in support services use over time, and the simultaneous use of different types of support services, are not well understood.[1]

This chapter examines services used by Illinois adult TANF leavers in the first year after exit. It draws on administrative records and survey data to describe statewide use patterns and to illustrate differing use patterns by region and service system.

Background on Support Services Use

Despite the fact that Medicaid and Food Stamp eligibility for working families does not necessarily end when TANF cases close, the caseloads for each of these programs declined nationally following welfare reform implementation (U.S. General Accounting Office, 1999a, 1999b). Food Stamp caseloads dropped more precipitously than Medicaid, and Medicaid reductions were concentrated among adults (Ku and Bruen, 1999; U.S. Department of Agriculture, 1999). Although a portion of such reductions may reflect

NEW DIRECTIONS FOR EVALUATION, no. 91, Fall 2001   © John Wiley & Sons, Inc.

reduced need, about two-thirds of former welfare families who stopped receiving Food Stamps met eligibility requirements (Zedlewski and Brauner, 1999).

These trends are consistent with research showing that low-income persons underuse many public programs. For example, the U.S. Department of Health and Human Services (2000) has estimated that only 12 percent of eligible recipients received federally supported child care in 1999. Pre-TANF studies also found underuse of the EITC, Medicaid, and child care services (Anderson, forthcoming; Ellwood and Adams, 1990; Hardina and Carley, 1997). Interview studies have found that underuse of these programs results primarily from lack of knowledge or confusion about eligibility rules (Anderson, forthcoming; Hardina and Carley, 1997; Stuber, Maloy, Rosenbaum, and Jones, 2000). Administrators and frontline service workers similarly have identified program complexity and confusion as barriers to service use (Ellwood, 1999; U.S. General Accounting Office, 1999b).

A Basic Support Services Package for TANF Leavers

Analyses of work-related support services often focus on a single service. However, it is useful to conceptualize a system or package of support services that collectively reinforces work efforts more broadly (Bane and Ellwood, 1994; Jencks, 1992). We consider here four support services commonly discussed from this perspective: the EITC, Food Stamps, Medicaid, and child care subsidies.

These programs represent an interesting mixture of cash, voucher, and service supports. The EITC is a federal tax credit that provides earnings supplements of up to $3,888 for families with two or more children and smaller credits for those with one child or who are childless. A person files for the EITC through the federal income tax system but need not owe federal taxes to receive the credit.

Food Stamps are coupons that are used to purchase food products in grocery stores. Although they are vouchers in a strict sense, they are treated as income in some measures due to their readily established cash value and easy liquidity. Because income eligibility cutoffs are higher for Food Stamps than for TANF, most TANF leavers continue to be eligible for some level of Food Stamps.

Medicaid and the related Children's Health Insurance Program (CHIP) expansions in the late 1980s and 1990s were responses to the inability of many low-wage workers to obtain private health insurance. All states are now required to provide transitional Medicaid assistance for six months to families that leave TANF due to increased earnings or work hours, and most states provide extensions in adult coverage beyond this period. Children are eligible for more extensive and non-time-limited coverage based on income. Illinois provides the transitional adult coverage for up to twelve months, as well as non-time-limited coverage for low-income children.

PRWORA did not mandate the provision of child care services for leavers, but increased federal child care funding was provided through a consolidated Child Care and Development Block Grant. Illinois provides non-time-limited child care to TANF leavers and other low-income persons with incomes up to 50 percent of the state median ($25,975 for a family of four), with recipient copayments based on income.

There are many other services for which some TANF leavers are eligible. These include Supplemental Security Income (SSI), the special supplemental food program Women, Infants, and Children (WIC), housing subsidies, and general assistance. A fuller exploration of use of this broader array of services by TANF leavers would be beneficial. Nonetheless, these services described represent a basic package available to assist the working poor as they make the transition from welfare to work, so analysis of how this set of services is used has important public policy implications.

Methods

The following data analyses rely on two complementary data sets. First, we examined Medicaid and Food Stamps use patterns in the first year after TANF exit, using Illinois Department of Human Services (IDHS) administrative data for cases that closed during the first eighteen months of the program: July 1997 to December 1998. The administrative records also included information on client characteristics, geographical location, and reasons for case closing.

Administrative data analyses were limited in several ways. Most important, data were not available on all services of interest. The administrative records also did not include information on the reasons that services were not used. These limitations aside, the administrative data offered the advantages of allowing longitudinal analyses of changes in service use, as well as sufficient numbers of cases to allow regional comparisons.

The administrative data shortcomings were alleviated through analysis of telephone interviews with a stratified random sample of 514 persons who left TANF in December 1998. The interviews were conducted six to eight months after the subjects left TANF. The survey response rate was 51 percent, and comparisons using administrative records indicated that survey respondents were similar to nonrespondents on important demographic variables. In addition to asking survey respondents if they were receiving selected support services, survey questions explored why leavers were not using each service. To avoid including cases that may have been closed temporarily, we limited both administrative and survey analysis to cases that remained closed for two consecutive months. Because our primary concern was determining how persons who left TANF used support services during periods when they were not on welfare, leavers who recidivated to TANF during the study period also were excluded. This prevents inflating estimates of service use by leavers, because recidivists almost always receive

Food Stamps and Medicaid when they return to TANF. After applying these exclusions, 78,346 leavers in the administrative data files and 419 survey interviews were available for analysis.

Findings

We begin by describing Medicaid and Food Stamp use patterns in the first year after exit, based on administrative data analysis.[2] Medicaid coverage was more common than Food Stamp use each month, and it followed a different longitudinal trend. Medicaid coverage ranged from 48 to 50 percent across the first four months after exit, and then steadily declined to 28 percent in the twelfth month after exit. In comparison, Food Stamp use remained between 22 and 23 percent each month.[3] The narrowing of use differences between these services may result partially from leavers reaching time limits for transitional Medicaid eligibility after six and twelve months.

Cumulative use patterns, which refer to the number of persons who ever use a service during a selected time period, illustrate that additional leavers depend on these services at some time in the first year after exit. Fifty-seven percent of the nonreturning leavers used Medicaid, and 39 percent used Food Stamps at some point during this first year (see Table 8.1).

Multiple Service Use Patterns. To explore multiple service use patterns, we first employ administrative data to analyze Food Stamp and Medicaid use in the first quarter and first year after exit. Table 8.1 reveals that fewer than one-fourth of nonreturning leavers used both of these services at some time in the quarter after exit, and only one-third used both during the first year. In comparison, 46 percent of leavers used neither of these services in the first quarter after exit, and 38 percent used neither in the first year. A large majority of the Food Stamp users also received Medicaid, as reflected by the small differences in cumulative use between those who received Food Stamps and those who received both services. However, many Medicaid users did not receive Food Stamps.

Table 8.1 also shows that use of these two services varied dramatically by geographic region. Use was substantially lower in Cook County, which includes Chicago, than in other geographical areas. For example, only 14 percent of Cook County nonreturning leavers received both Food Stamps and Medicaid in the quarter after exit, as compared with over 40 percent of those in rural areas.

Because it includes information on child care and EITC use, the survey data allow more detailed analysis of multiple service use, but only for a single time point. Leavers were asked if they were receiving Food Stamps, Medicaid, and child care subsidies when interviewed. The EITC is received only once a year, so leavers were asked if they previously had received the credit.

Table 8.2 shows use patterns by nonreturning surveyed leavers for selected subsets of these four services. In addition to the complete set, the table shows use patterns for a social service system–administered package

Table 8.1. Food Stamp and Medicaid Use by Nonreturning Leavers (Administrative Data)

Region	Use of Food Stamps and/ or Medicaid in Quarter after Exit (in percent)				Use of Food Stamps and/ or Medicaid in Year after Exit (in percent)			
	Food Stamps	Medicaid	Both	Neither	Food Stamps	Medicaid	Both	Neither
Cook (n=39,402)	17.8	43.0	13.8	53.0	29.8	49.8	24.1	44.5
Suburban Metro. (n=6,954)	25.4	52.9	23.0	44.7	38.2	60.8	34.9	36.0
Downstate Urban (n=16,726)	32.4	54.5	28.5	41.6	45.5	61.8	40.1	32.9
Rural North (n=10,838)	43.9	63.9	40.9	33.1	56.5	71.4	52.5	24.6
Rural South (n=4,466)	45.9	59.6	41.4	35.9	57.9	67.3	52.4	27.1
Illinois Total (n=78,386)	26.8	50.2	23.0	46.1	39.2	57.3	34.0	37.5

(Medicaid, Food Stamps, and child care), a service-related package (Medicaid and child care), an income-related package (Food Stamps and the EITC), and the Food Stamps and Medicaid package.

Only 3 percent of survey leavers were using the complete set of services, and only 16 percent were using three or more services. Few leavers were using all of the services in the other defined service packages (see the boldface type). In comparison, 74 percent were using at least one of these services. Taken together, these data suggest that widespread packaging of most available supports is uncommon. However, total independence from government supports also is not the norm six to eight months after exit.

Reasons for Nonuse of Support Services. In exploring reasons for the relatively low levels of service use among leavers, we first present survey data on leaver-reported reasons for nonuse. Logistic regression analysis based on the administrative data then is presented to assess factors associated with Medicaid and Food Stamp use.

Survey Data on Reasons for Nonuse. Table 8.3 provides survey responses on reasons for nonuse of Medicaid and Food Stamps. The top portion of the table shows three distinct subgroups among those who were not receiving

Table 8.2. Packages of Service Supports Used by Nonreturning TANF Leavers, Six to Eight Months After TANF Exit (Survey Data)

	Number of Services Used (percentage of all leavers, n=419)				
Benefit Package	None	One	Two	Three	Four
Medicaid, Food Stamps, child care, EITC	26.3	33.1	24.9	13.0	**2.6**
Medicaid, Food Stamps, child care	46.3	26.8	22.7	**4.2**	N.A.
Medicaid, Food Stamps	53.6	27.1	**19.3**	N.A.	N.A.
Medicaid, child care	52.1	37.1	**10.7**	N.A.	N.A.
EITC, Food Stamps	38.8	48.3	**12.9**	N.A.	N.A.

Note: Boldface type indicates use of all services in the indicated benefit package.

these services: those who had received the service after exit but were not using it when interviewed, those who applied for it but had not received the service, and those who had not applied for the service. Two points are noteworthy from this information. First, most leavers not using these services when interviewed had not used them at any time since leaving TANF; only 22 percent of Medicaid nonusers and 15 percent of Food Stamp nonusers had received these services at any time since exiting TANF. Second, among those who had not received a service since leaving, the vast majority had not applied. Consequently, the dominant subgroup among nonusers, representing 61 percent of Medicaid and 72 percent of Food Stamp nonusers, were those who had not applied for these services.

The bottom portion of the table presents coded open-ended responses on reasons for nonuse among those who had not applied. Four response categories were most common. First, over one-third of Medicaid nonusers and about one-fourth of Food Stamp nonusers indicated they did not need the service. In addition, about one-tenth of each group said that they did not want the service, usually because of a desire for independence.

A third group, representing 23 percent of Medicaid and 31 percent of Food Stamp nonusers, either did not know about the possibility for eligibility or else thought they would not be eligible. Finally, 16 percent of Medicaid and 25 percent of Food Stamp nonusers suggested that applying for these services was too much of a hassle or too time-consuming. Combining these latter two groups, about 40 percent of Medicaid and 56 percent of Food Stamp nonusers had not applied either because of perceived ineligibility or systems constraints.

Table 8.3. Reasons for Nonuse of Medicaid and Food Stamps by Nonreturning Leavers, at Time of Interview

Patterns Of Nonuse for Leavers Not Receiving Service When Interviewed

	Medicaid		Food Stamps	
	% of All Leavers (n=419)	% of Those Not Now Receiving Service (n=254)	% of All Leavers (n=419)	% of Those Not Now Receiving Service (n=309)
Receiving now	39.4	N.A.	26.2	N.A.
Received since leaving, but not now	13.1	21.7	11.2	15.2
Have not received since leaving	47.5	78.3	62.6	84.8
Applied	10.7	17.7	9.5	12.9
Not applied	36.8	60.6	53.0	71.8

Reasons for Nonuse for Leavers Who Have Not Used or Applied for the Service Since Exit

	% of Medicaid Nonusers(n=141)	% of Food Stamps Nonusers (n=216)
Not needed	35.4	23.6
Not wanted	9.9	8.8
Did not know about or believe eligible for	23.4	31.0
Too much hassle or time	16.3	24.5
Other	14.9	12.0

Reasons offered for nonuse of child care subsidies also suggest that both lack of need and lack of knowledge were important factors. While 62 percent of survey leavers in work or training activities used paid child care, only 42 percent of these received public child care subsidies. Of those who paid for care but did not receive public support, half either did not know about government child care subsidies or else thought they were ineligible for them. Those who did not obtain subsidies had monthly out-of-pocket costs that were nearly twice as high as those who did ($267 versus $142).

The remaining 38 percent of leavers in work or training activities either left their children alone or used unpaid child care arrangements. Over 87 percent of the leavers who had others care for their children expressed satisfaction with such arrangements, suggesting that use of unpaid care does not necessarily indicate unmet need. In fact, only 18 percent of leavers using unpaid child care arrangements indicated that they had unmet child care needs.

Finally, nonuse of the EITC most often resulted from lack of knowledge. Fifty-five percent of leavers indicated that they had not received this credit. Of these, only one-third had even a vague idea of what the credit was. One might hypothesize that because the EITC is available only to those who work, lack of knowledge may result from the nonworking status of many leavers. However, although knowledge about the EITC varied significantly by consistency of employment since TANF exit (χ = 12.6; df = 2; p < .01), lack of knowledge was not limited to nonworkers. In fact, 86 percent of those who did not know about the credit had worked at least some since leaving TANF, and one-third had worked consistently.

Factors Associated with Service Use. Logistic regression was used to estimate the effects of selected factors on Food Stamps and Medicaid use by nonreturning leavers in the first year after exit. Logistic regression allows the estimation of the effects of a set of independent variables on a binominal dependent variable. The independent variables included in these analyses were limited by the data included in the administrative records. However, these records include many variables that hypothetically may affect service use.

Two independent variables were included to explore whether administrative variations affect service use. First, the closing reason indicates whether the case closed for income, noncooperation, or other reasons. Second, five geographic regions were compared, based on the hypothesis that staffing competencies, administrative practices, or caseload levels may differ among welfare offices in each region.

Human capital and wage factors were measured by whether the leaver completed high school and had employment experience, as well as wage levels in the quarter before exit and quarter of exit. Race, age of leaver, presence of children in selected age groups, and welfare spell length were entered as demographic variables. A cohort variable also was included to control for possible differences between monthly leaver cohorts.

Table 8.4 presents the results of the Food Stamp regression. The model chi-square statistic presented in the table indicates that the model is statistically significant. Logistic regression allows the presentation of odds ratios, which represent the relative probability of the occurrence of the dependent variable. In the table, the odds ratios compare the probability of using Food Stamps in the first year after exit for a given variable category, when compared with an excluded or baseline category that by definition has an odds ratio of 1.0. The excluded categories are shown in parentheses in Table 8.4 whenever appropriate.

The findings suggest the importance of the administratively related variables in explaining service use. When holding other model factors constant, a leaver in Cook County (Chicago and surrounding inner suburbs) was only one-fourth as likely to receive Food Stamps as leavers in the rural north region, and those in suburban Chicago and downstate urban counties were only 45 percent and 56 percent, respectively, as likely to receive Food Stamps.[4]

The closing reason also significantly affected Food Stamp receipt. Those who closed for income-related reasons were 72 percent more likely to use

Table 8.4. Logistic Regression Effects on Food Stamp Use in the First Year After TANF Exit

Characteristic	Coefficient	Standard error	Odds ratio
Intercept	0.510*	0.037	
Exit reason (compared with other reasons)			
Exited due to income	0.543*	0.019	1.72
Exited due to noncooperation	−0.785*	0.022	0.46
Demographics			
African American (compared with white)	0.472*	0.021	1.60
Hispanic (compared with white)	0.050	0.032	1.05
Child <1 (compared with those having no child under age 1)	−0.150*	0.030	0.86
Child 1–5 (compared with those having no child aged 1–5)	−0.066*	0.020	0.94
Child 6–12 (compared with those having no child aged 6–12)	−0.148*	0.024	0.86
Age < 16 (compared with those 31+)	−0.241	0.292	0.79
Age 17–19 (compared with those 31+)	−0.242*	0.043	0.79
Age 20–25 (compared with those 31+)	−0.328*	0.022	0.72
Age 26–30 (compared with those 31+)	−0.237*	0.022	0.79
Never married (compared with married, divorce, or separated)	−0.006	0.019	1.01
Time on welfare before exit	0.006*	0.000	1.01
Education and employment			
High school graduate or more	−0.154*	0.018	0.86
Professional/manager (compared with no experience)	−0.238*	0.052	0.79
Clerical (compared with no xperience)	−0.172*	0.033	0.84
Sales (compared with no experience)	−0.162*	0.048	0.85
Crafts/operator (compared with no experience)	−0.069	0.046	0.93
Service (compared with no experience)	−0.044	0.023	0.96
Laborer (compared with no experience)	−0.077*	0.026	0.93
Wages in quarter before exit	−0.000*	0.000	1.00
Wages in quarter of exit	−0.000*	0.000	1.00
Region (compared with rural north)			
Cook County	−1.378*	0.029	0.25
Suburban counties	−0.801*	0.035	0.45
Downstate urban	−0.581*	0.027	0.56
Rural south	0.021	0.038	1.02
Control variable			
Cohort	-0.012	0.002	1.01

*p < .05

−2 log likelihood: 100951.3

Model Chi-square 9064.8, df(27), p < .0001

Number of observations: 75,296

Food Stamps than leavers closing for other reasons, which included reasons such as moving, inability to locate, and children no longer being eligible for TANF. In comparison, cases closed for noncooperation were only 46 percent as likely to receive Food Stamps as leavers closed for other reasons. This relatively lower use by leavers closed for noncooperation reasons may result partially from intended policy, as cases closed for failure to report income have their Food Stamp cases closed for the same reason. However, most TANF cases closed for noncooperation are closed for other reasons, such as failure to keep employment and training-related appointments, and such closures should not automatically be accompanied by Food Stamp closings.

One may hypothesize that those with more education and work experience will be less likely to use Food Stamps, assuming that these human capital characteristics translate into greater self-sufficiency. However, it also is possible that lower education levels may discourage service use, particularly if eligibility rules are difficult to understand. The findings in Table 8.4 show that those who finished high school were slightly but significantly less likely to use Food Stamps, as were leavers with experience in four of the six occupational categories.

Finally, some demographic differences are noteworthy. African American leavers were somewhat more likely to use Food Stamps than white leavers, and users in younger age groups (excluding those age sixteen and younger) were significantly less likely to use Food Stamps than leavers aged thirty-one and over. Differences in use by age of children were small but statistically significant.

Because Illinois achieved nearly universal Medicaid coverage for leavers who closed for income reasons, the regression run for Medicaid use included only leavers who left for reasons other than income. The regional effects were similar to those for Food Stamps, and cases closed for noncooperation again were much less likely to receive Medicaid. There were no significant racial differences in Medicaid use, but cases with children aged one through five or six through twelve were significantly more likely to receive Medicaid, as were adult teenage leavers. Leavers who finished high school also were significantly more likely to receive Medicaid in the first year after exit.

Conclusion

The findings demonstrate the importance of support services to TANF leavers. Nearly two-thirds of all nonreturning leavers used either Food Stamps or Medicaid at some point in the first year after exit. This fairly high degree of service use may be overlooked in studies that examine use of single services at single time points.

Nonetheless, leavers rarely packaged support services in the manner envisioned in public policy discussions about transitional supports after welfare. This incomplete use pattern is consistent with the traditional residual character of the American welfare state, in which services are provided in response to specific deficits rather than as basic entitlements in support of agreed-on living standards (Gilbert and Terrell, 1998). Such a residual service model may be acceptable to policy analysts if it reflects consistent and equitable determinations of need. However, in this study, many seemingly eligible leavers did not receive services, and nonusers most often did not indicate a lack of need.

Administrative practices appeared to play an important role in support service use variations. Although local IDHS offices operate under uniform state policies regarding the support services examined, administrative data analysis revealed that recipients in rural areas were much more likely to receive Food Stamps and Medicaid than were leavers in other areas, particularly when other variables were controlled. In addition, survey responses indicated that non-service-using recipients often did not understand eligibility rules or else viewed applying for services as burdensome.

Research that examines levels of support service use under varying service delivery models therefore is needed. Variations in caseworker roles in developing service plans for TANF recipients and leavers should be included in such efforts. Attention to service eligibility rules and administrative practices associated with different case closing circumstances would be especially useful. The intent would be to determine if varying use patterns among those whose cases close for different reasons reflect intended or unintended actions.

These issues will grow in importance as TANF time limits are reached. As persons with marginal skills exhaust TANF assistance, receipt of a range of support services will be critical in reinforcing work efforts and preventing destitution. Ensuring that policies and related administrative practices maximize the probability that agreed-on services are accessible represents an important challenge for both researchers and public administrators.

Notes

1. The term *support services*, rather than *benefits*, is used throughout this chapter, even though the EITC and Food Stamps are not services in a technical sense. We make this choice to maintain consistency with the intended purposes of these programs to support low-wage work efforts.

2. The Medicaid data refer to whether a leaver had Medicaid coverage, as opposed to whether that coverage was used to obtain medical services during the period in question. For simplicity of presentation, we at times refer to Medicaid coverage as use in data presentations.

3. The administrative data set does not include special one-month issuances that are provided to most TANF leavers who are not continued on the regular Food Stamp rolls. This leads to an understatement of Food Stamp use, mainly in the month of exit and the month following exit. However, this shortcoming in the data decreases over time, as persons who receive the one-month issuances will reapply and appear on the regular rolls or else drop off. Comparisons of the administrative data and the survey data also indicate consistency in use rates between these two data sources.

4. The term *likely* is used loosely here. An odds ratio of .25 means that the odds that an individual in Chicago receives Food Stamps are one-fourth that of an individual living in the rural north of Illinois. The difference in the predicted probabilities would depend on the probability that an individual in the rural north received Food Stamps.

References

Anderson, S. "Assuring the Stability of Welfare to Work Exits: The Importance of Recipient Knowledge About Work Incentives." *Social Work,* forthcoming.

Bane, M. J., and Ellwood, D. T. *Welfare Realities: From Rhetoric to Reform.* Cambridge, Mass.: Harvard University Press, 1994.

Danziger, S. H. "Introduction." In S. H. Danziger (ed.), *Economic Conditions and Welfare Reform.* Kalamazoo, Mich.: W. E. Upjohn Institute for Employment Research, 1999.

Ellwood, M. *The Medicaid Eligibility Maze: Coverage Expands, But Enrollment Problems Persist.* Washington, D.C.: Urban Institute, 1999.

Ellwood, D. T., and Adams, E. K. "Medicaid Mysteries: Transitional Benefits, Medicaid Coverage, and Welfare Exits." *Health Care Financing Review/1990 Annual Supplement,* 1990, pp. 119–131.

Gilbert, N., and Terrell, P. *Dimensions of Social Policy.* (4th ed.) Needham Heights, Mass.: Allyn & Bacon, 1998.

Hardina, D., and Carley, M. "The Impact of Increased Allowable Work Hours on Two-Parent Families Receiving Welfare." *Social Work Research,* 1997, *21,* 101–109.

Jencks, C. *Rethinking Social Policy: Race, Poverty, and the Underclass.* Cambridge, Mass.: Harvard University Press, 1992.

Ku, L., and Bruen, B. *The Continuing Decline in Medicaid Coverage.* Washington, D.C.: Urban Institute, 1999.

Loprest, P. *Families Who Left Welfare: Who Are They and How Are They Doing?* Washington, D.C.: Urban Institute, 1999.

Stuber, J., Maloy, K., Rosenbaum, S., and Jones, K. *Beyond Stigma: What Barriers Actually Affect the Decisions of Low-Income Families to Enroll in Medicaid?* Washington, D.C.: Center for Health Services Research and Policy, George Washington University Medical Center, 2000.

U.S. Department of Agriculture. Food and Nutrition Service. *Who Is Leaving the Food Stamp Program: An Analysis of Caseload Changes from 1994 to 1998.* Washington, D.C.: U.S. Department of Agriculture, 1999.

U.S. Department of Health and Human Services. Administration for Children and Families. "New Statistics Show Only Small Percentage of Eligible Families Receive Child Care Help." *HHS News.* [www.acf.dhhs.gov/news/ccstudy.htm]. 2000.

U.S. General Accounting Office. *Food Stamp Program: Various Factors Have Led to Declining Participation.* Washington, D.C.: U.S. General Accounting Office, 1999a.

U.S. General Accounting Office. *Medicaid Enrollment: Amid Declines, State Efforts to Ensure Coverage After Welfare Vary.* Washington, D.C.: U.S. General Accounting Office 1999b.

Zedlewski, S. R., and Brauner, S. *Declines in Food Stamp and Welfare Participation: Is There a Connection?* Washington, D.C.: Urban Institute, 1999.

Steven G. Anderson *is an assistant professor at the School of Social Work, University of Illinois at Urbana-Champaign.*

Anthony P. Halter *is an associate professor at the School of Social Work, University of Illinois at Urbana-Champaign.*

Richard Schuldt *is the director of the Survey Research Office, University of Illinois at Springfield.*

9

This chapter examines the degree of self-sufficiency and the need for sustained income supports among leavers in Missouri.

Continuing Use of Low-Income Services by Former Missouri Welfare Recipients

Nancy Dunton, Jane Mosley, Lola Butcher

The sweeping nature of the Personal Responsibility and Work Opportunity Reconciliation Act of 1996 (PRWORA) presented a challenge to evaluating the effects of welfare reform on individuals, programs, and local communities. As with any other major social change, there were both theoretical and practical concerns about intended and unintended consequences. Of specific interest to this chapter were the concerns about whether needy families would continue to have access to and use transitional services and low-income support programs such as Food Stamps, Medicaid, and subsidized child care. In addition, it was feared that there might be a cost shift from the federal government to local communities if families who lost benefits under welfare reform would turn instead to community-based emergency assistance.

Missouri's Temporary Assistance to Needy Families program (TANF), called Temporary Assistance, is designed to provide assistance to needy families with children so that they can be cared for in their own home and to reduce dependency by promoting job preparation, work, and marriage. Following are the major provisions:

Able-bodied adult cash assistance recipients must work or be in work activities (job training, subsidized employment, job search, or job readiness assistance) after two years of receiving assistance. This provision is subject to good cause exemptions on a limited basis.
Receipt of cash assistance under Temporary Assistance is restricted to a lifetime limit of five years.

New Directions for Evaluation, no. 91, Fall 2001 © John Wiley & Sons, Inc.

As of fiscal year 2000, individuals receiving cash assistance (unless exempt) must work at least thirty hours per week (averaged over a month) to be counted toward meeting the work participation rate.

An assessment of the effects of welfare reform on former Missouri welfare recipients has shown that some of the primary goals of reform have been achieved. Specifically, most former recipients have shown a substantial and sustained attachment to the labor force (Mosley, Dunton, and Butcher, 2001). However, most former recipients also have low household incomes and remain eligible for services targeted to low-income families. Some of these services generally were thought of as transitional services for former cash assistance recipients, while others target all low-income households. The Missouri study has shown that for as long as two and a half years after exit, most former welfare recipients continued to use a variety of non-cash assistance programs. This situation raises questions about the degree of self-sufficiency achieved by former cash assistance recipients and the need for sustained income supports for low-income households. This chapter addresses these questions using data produced in the assessment of Missouri's welfare reform initiative.[1]

Methodology

The data used in this study were derived from three sources: a survey of former Missouri welfare recipients (leavers), administrative data on low-income supports from the Department of Social Services, and, for Kansas City only, data on the use of emergency assistance provided by community-based organizations.

Survey Data. Much of the information needed to examine the well-being of leavers is not available through administrative sources. Therefore, we conducted a survey of a sample of twelve hundred adult leavers who left Aid to Families with Dependent Children (AFDC) in the fourth quarter of 1996.[2] Interviews were conducted in the spring and summer of 1999, more than two and a half years after exit, at a time when the state's unemployment rate was low (3.4 percent). The survey achieved a 75 percent response rate.[3] In addition, there was no evidence that respondents differed from nonrespondents on key indicators (see Dunton, Mosley, and Butcher, 2001, for more information). The questionnaire elicited information in ten topical modules, among them work effort, earnings, household income, and the need for and use of various types of government and nongovernment assistance.

State Administrative Data. Data on the receipt of government services targeted to low-income populations were obtained from the state's administrative records and merged to the survey records prior to analysis. Records were obtained for the following programs: TANF, Medicaid, Food Stamps, and child care assistance. Sample members were identified in these records on the basis of their former case identifier, which is constant across time and program. For those who remained in Missouri, administrative data were considered more reliable than survey data on the current receipt of services.[4]

Data on Community-Based Emergency Assistance. We obtained data on the use of community-based emergency assistance in the Kansas City metropolitan area[5] by drawing on a unique local database maintained by the Mid America Assistance Coalition (MAAC), a nonprofit organization that coordinates all types of community assistance in the Kansas City area.[6] Its database contains approximately 1.1 million service records from 167 community-based organizations. MAAC officials believe the database covers approximately 90 percent of all community assistance provided in the Kansas City area since 1994. The database contains the name and social security number of the recipient and the date, types, and value of the service received.[7] We examined receipt of food and consumer items and of utility, transportation, and housing assistance provided by community-based organizations. This portion of the analysis was based on all persons in the 1996 exit cohort who resided in the Kansas City urban counties (Jackson, Clay, and Platte Counties) at the time of exit, not just the sample from that cohort selected for the survey. Records were identified by using the social security number of the adult leaver. MAAC records were linked to state administrative records on TANF and Food Stamps for the period from 1996 to 1999 on the basis of the leaver's social security number.

Findings: Continuing Use of Government Supports

Most leavers had low household incomes and remained eligible for many services targeted to low-income families.[8] The median income in leaver households was $1,166 per month, placing 58 percent of them below the poverty line. Moreover, 90 percent had incomes that classified them as poor or near poor. Over a quarter of the households were classified as living in extreme poverty.[9] Since leaving assistance, almost half of the leavers had returned to TANF for some period.[10] Fourteen percent were receiving TANF at the time of the survey.

Medicaid and Child Health Insurance Program. Many individuals in leaver households were covered by public health insurance two and a half years after exit from public assistance: 65 percent of these households reported that Medicaid and Child Health Insurance Program (CHIP) covered at least one member, and children were much more likely to have Medicaid/CHIP coverage than were adults.[11] One-third of leavers were covered by Medicaid, and 68 percent of children were enrolled in the program (see Table 9.1).

Food Stamps. The Food Stamp program was a common form of government assistance received by leavers. Over 80 percent had used Food Stamps since exiting AFDC two and a half years earlier. Just under half of the leavers were using Food Stamps at the time of the survey, but this accounts for only 60 percent of those we estimated to be eligible.[12]

**Table 9.1. Health Insurance Coverage, Former Missouri
AFDC Recipients**

Coverage Source	Adults (%)	Children (%)
Medicaid/CHIP	33	68
Employer or spouse/partner's		
employer	29	20
Other source	5	3
No health insurance	32	8
N	878	1578

Source: Missouri Leavers' Survey

Eligible households that did not receive Food Stamps at the time of the survey were better off financially than those that did (see Table 9.2). Median income of nonrecipients was 40 percent higher than that among recipients. The large income difference between the two groups suggests that the neediest of welfare leavers were applying for and receiving Food Stamps.

Households that received Food Stamps also had much higher receipt of other forms of assistance. At the time of the survey, one-quarter of recip-

**Table 9.2. Characteristics of Families by Food Stamp Receipt,
Households Under 130 Percent of the Poverty Line**

	Received Food Stamps in Last Month	
	Yes	No
Median household income	$630	$1,060
Work history		
Currently working	50%	65%
Formerly worked	38%	23%
Never worked	12%	12%
No high school diploma or GED	42%	25%
Presence of spouse/partner	21%	42%
Received TANF in last month	26%	5%
Household included Medicaid		
recipient	90%	53%
Months on TANF, 1997–1999	6.7	3.8
Months on AFDC, 1992–1996	29	28
Months on Food Stamps, 1997–1999	12.9	5.6
Unable to buy enough food in		
last month	25%	37%
Had a child skip meals in last month	2%	6%
Unable to pay rent, mortgage,		
or utilities	35%	23%
N	371	294

Source: Missouri Leavers' Survey; Missouri administrative records.

ients also received TANF, and 90 percent had someone in the household covered by Medicaid. Moreover, those currently receiving Food Stamps had been on TANF and Food Stamps more months since the 1996 exit than those who were not receiving Food Stamps at the time of the survey. While it has been suggested that receipt of TANF or Medicaid could serve as a gateway to the Food Stamp program, recall that more than 80 percent of all leaver households had received Food Stamps since exiting AFDC. Thus, most families should have had some awareness of the program and approximate eligibility levels.

Despite their relatively better economic status, eligible households that did not receive Food Stamps reported a greater unmet need for food assistance. More than one-third (37 percent) of the nonrecipient households stated that there had been a time in the previous month when they were unable to buy enough food for their needs compared with a quarter of the Food Stamp households. Similarly, 6 percent of the nonrecipient households noted that their children had skipped meals in the previous month because of lack of food, compared with just 2 percent of recipient households. Food Stamps probably ameliorated deprivation in recipient households.

Child Care. From administrative records, we know that there was relatively little use of child care subsidies among leavers. We estimated eligibility for child care subsidies based on household income, age of children, and work or education activities of the leaver.[13] At the time of the survey, one-quarter (28 percent) of those eligible were using a subsidy, and over half (55 percent) had used child care subsidies in the two and a half years since leaving AFDC.

Several characteristics distinguished eligible leavers who used subsidies from those who did not (see Table 9.3). According to the survey data, leavers who used subsidies were less well educated and less likely to have a spouse or partner. Households with subsidies contained younger children, which may indicate a greater potential child care expense. They were also much more likely to have relied on Food Stamps in the prior month, and in more months since exit, than eligible households without subsidies, despite our finding no difference between these two groups in median income.

Housing. The survey asked about the use of two types of housing assistance: public housing and Section 8 subsidies.[14] One-quarter (26 percent) of the sample was receiving housing assistance at the time of the survey: 12 percent were receiving Section 8, and 14 percent were in public housing.[15]

There were several differences between leavers who were and those who were not receiving housing assistance when surveyed (see Table 9.4). Income was one of the most striking differences, with those receiving assistance having median incomes that were just half that of those who were not receiving assistance. Leavers with housing assistance were also more likely to have received TANF in the past month and received more months of Food Stamps since exit, and were less likely to have been working at the time of the survey. Those receiving housing assistance were also much less likely to have a spouse or partner. Interestingly, education level was remarkably similar across the groups.

Table 9.3. Household Characteristics by Receipt of Child Care Assistance: Eligible Households and Former Missouri AFDC Recipients, Employed Leavers Only

	Received Child Care Assistance at Time of Survey	
	Yes	No
Household income (median)	$1,000	$1,000
No high school diploma or GED	21%	37%
Presence of spouse/partner	7%	23%
Received TANF in last month	5%	10%
Received Food Stamps in last month	69%	47%
Household included Medicaid recipient	90%	70%
Months on TANF, 1997–1999	4.0	4.6
Months on AFDC, 1992–1996	36	28
Months on Food Stamps, 1997–1999	12.7	8.4
Age of youngest child	4	6
N	75	200

Source: Missouri Leavers' Survey; Missouri administrative records.

Women, Infants, and Children Program. Overall, less than one-quarter of leavers reported in the survey that they were receiving WIC. WIC recipients were also more likely than their counterparts to have received TANF in the last month. Fewer WIC recipients had a high school diploma than nonrecipients. However, there were only trivial differences in household income between WIC recipients and those who did not receive WIC. Rates of receipt were highest among those who were not currently working but had worked since leaving cash assistance (former or intermittent workers). The Missouri study repeatedly found that intermittent workers were more economically vulnerable than leavers who were working at the time of the survey or those who had not worked since exit (Mosley, Dunton, and Butcher, 2001).

Multiple Types of Assistance. Many leavers were using one or more types of assistance. When looking across six programs (TANF, Medicaid, Food Stamps, child care subsidies, housing assistance, and WIC) using linked survey and administrative data, we found that more than 75 percent of leavers were relying on one or more types of assistance at the time of the survey (see Table 9.6).[16] One-third of the sample were using three or more kinds of assistance.

The most common type of assistance received was Medicaid/CHIP. Of those leavers receiving only one type of assistance, 63 percent received Medicaid (see Table 9.7). In addition, for leavers who received more than one benefit, Medicaid were almost always part of the assistance package.

TANF was almost always used in combination with other kinds of assistance. Those receiving TANF were receiving on average between three and four benefits (including TANF). For households receiving two benefits,

Table 9.4. Household Characteristics by Receipt of Housing Assistance: Survey Data Only, Former Missouri AFDC Recipients

	Received Housing Assistance When Surveyed	
	Yes	No
Household income (median)	$650	$1,235
Work history		
Currently working	61%	67%
Formerly worked	31%	23%
Never worked	8%	10%
No high school diploma or GED	35%	32%
Presence of spouse/partner	8%	41%
Receipt of TANF in last month	24%	11%
Receipt of Food Stamps in last month	74%	38%
Household contained Medicaid recipient	80%	59%
Months on TANF, 1997–1999	6.4	4.9
Months on AFDC, 1992–1996	26	28
Months on Food Stamps, 1997–1999	12.3	7.4
N	217	657

Source: Missouri Leavers' Survey.

Table 9.5. Household Characteristics by Receipt of WIC: Survey Data Only, Former Missouri AFDC Recipients

	Received WIC When Surveyed	
	Yes	No
Household income (median)	$1,000	$1,150
Work history		
Currently employed	56%	68%
Formerly employed	33%	23%
Never employed	11%	9%
No high school diploma or GED	42%	30%
Presence of spouse/partner	36%	31%
Receipt of TANF in last month	24%	13%
Receipt of Food Stamps in last month	61%	43%
Household contained Medicaid recipient	82%	60%
Months on TANF, 1997–1999	6	4
Months on AFDC, 1992–1996	30	28
Months on Food Stamps, 1997–1999	10	8
N	201	677

Source: Missouri Leavers' Survey.

Note: Only households with children under the age of six were asked about WIC receipt.

Table 9.6. Number of Benefits Received at Time of Survey: Former Missouri AFDC Recipients

Number of Benefits	Percentage Receiving
0	25
1	18
2	23
3	17
4+	17
N	878

the most common combinations of benefits included Medicaid. Over half received Food Stamps and Medicaid. Seventeen percent used Medicaid and WIC, and 10 percent received Medicaid and child care subsidies.

We also examined the characteristics of families receiving different numbers of benefits (see Table 9.8). As expected, as the number of benefits received rose, median income declined. Other factors that were generally associated with income, such as education level and presence of a spouse or partner, also were inversely related to the number of benefits received. In addition, intermittent workers were disproportionately represented among those with more benefits.

Findings: Use of Community-Based Emergency Assistance

Low-income households often rely on assistance from a variety of sources. Government provides many types of assistance to these families. According to the survey results, family and friends were a frequent source of assistance (Mosley, Dunton, and Butcher, 2001). Community-based

Table 9.7. Type and Number of Benefits Received: Former Missouri AFDC Recipients

	1 Source (%)	2 Sources (%)	3 Sources (%)	4 or More Sources (%)
Medicaid	63	90	93	97
Food Stamps	13	60	84	97
Child care	2	10	15	45
Public housing	11	16	48	71
WIC	11	20	34	59
TANF	1	5	26	49
N	174	200	139	150

Source: Missouri Leavers' Survey; Missouri administrative records.

Table 9.8. Household Characteristics by Number of Types of Benefits Received: Former Missouri AFDC Recipients

	Number of Benefits Received When Surveyed				
	0	*1*	*2*	*3*	*4 or more*
Household income	$1,650	$1,263	$963	$890	$603
Work history					
Currently working	78%	74%	69%	56%	46%
Intermittent worker	14%	16%	23%	32%	43%
Never worked	8%	10%	9%	13%	11%
No high school					
diploma or GED	19%	36%	35%	35%	43%
Presence of spouse/					
partner	46%	45%	30%	18%	14%
Months on TANF,					
1997–1999	2.8	4.0	4.3	7.3	8.5
Months on AFDC,					
1992–1996	27	27	27	30	25
Months on Food					
Stamps, 1997–1999	3.0	6.5	10.3	12.5	13.3
N	215	174	200	139	150

Source: Missouri Leavers' Survey; Missouri Income Maintenance Files and other administrative records.

organizations are also part of the safety net. To the extent that welfare leavers transfer their reliance from governmental assistance to community-based organizations, the goals of welfare reform will not be met. We were able to address this question for the Kansas City area using the MAAC database. We examined the MAAC data for all those who resided in the three Kansas City metropolitan counties who exited AFDC in the fourth quarter of 1996.

Nearly half of Kansas City leavers relied on some form of community-based emergency assistance following their 1996 exit from AFDC. Clearly, community-based assistance is important to a large segment of leavers. Nevertheless, most of these leavers used community assistance only sporadically. Among the leavers who received any assistance, the average was 2.3 services per year, and the median was less than one per year.[17]

Another way to assess reliance on MAAC services is by the total dollar value of services received.[18] Among leavers who received services, the median value was just $97 per year (see Table 9.9). However, values varied widely depending on the type of service received; for example, the average value of one utility assistance benefit was $130, compared with $40 for the average food benefit.

We also assessed whether there was an increase in leavers' use of community-based assistance after their exit from AFDC, relative to their

Table 9.9. Annual Value of Services Received by Former Kansas City AFDC Recipients, 1997–2000

	All Leavers	Leavers with Receipt After Exit
25th percentile	$0	$38
50th percentile	$0	$97
75th percentile	$97	$220
N	1,932	942

Source: Mid America Assistance Coalition MAACLink database.

use prior to exit. A slightly higher percentage of leavers used MAAC services after exit than in the three years prior to exit (see Table 9.10). However, for leavers who used MAAC assistance, the number of benefits was very similar in the two time periods; in fact, the means and medians were identical.

Although the frequency of use did not increase after exit, the average value of MAAC services did increase by more than 40 percent, from $97 in the pre-exit period to $143 in the post-exit period. Nevertheless, the annual value was still relatively small and would not be sufficient to replace the value of public supports, such as TANF or Food Stamps.

As shown in Table 9.11, the services most commonly received were food, followed by consumer items and utility aid. Only a small percentage of leavers received rent assistance or transportation assistance.

Table 9.10. MAAC Service Receipt: Former Kansas City AFDC Recipients

	1994–1996 (Pre-exit)	1997–2000 (Post-exit)
All leavers		
No use	57%	51%
N	1932	1932
Leavers who used assistance Annual number of services		
0.33 to 1	38%	40%
1 to 2	25%	22%
2 or more	37%	38%
Mean	2.9	2.9
Median	1.4	1.4
N	823	942

Source: Mid America Assistance Coalition, MAACLink database

Table 9.11. Type of Community Assistance Used, January 1997–May 2000: Former Kansas City AFDC Recipients

	Percent Receiving
Food	41
Consumer items	32
Utilities	24
Housing	7
Transportation	2
N	1932

Source: Mid America Assistance Coalition MAACLink database

Both administrative and survey data suggest that emergency assistance users were needier than nonusers were. Nonusers made less use of government services (see Table 9.12).[20] They had lower rates of returns to TANF and spent fewer months on TANF and Food Stamps. Differences between less and more frequent users were less pronounced.

Additional information on the characteristics of emergency assistance users was available for the one out of ten Kansas City leavers who were included in the survey (see Table 9.13). While based on relatively small numbers, these data show that more frequent users were half as likely as nonusers to be living with a spouse or partner, were less likely to have a high school diploma, were less likely to be currently working, had lower incomes, and had higher levels of food deprivation.

Table 9.12. Use of Public Assistance by Post-Exit MAAC Recipients: Former Kansas City Area AFDC Recipients

Number of Services:	No Use	*Less than 1 Service per Year*	*More than 1 Service per Year*
Percentage returning to TANF after exit	25[a, b]	40[b]	53
Months on TANF, 1997–1998	2.5[a, b]	4.2[b]	5.9
Months on Food Stamps, 1997–1998	3.9[a, b]	6.1[b]	8.6
Months on AFDC, 1992–1996	25[a, b]	30	28
N	990	380	562

Source: Mid America Assistance Coalition MAACLink database; Missouri administrative records.
[a]Significantly different from group 2 at the .05 level.
[b]Significantly different from group 3 at the .05 level.

Table 9.13. Demographic Characteristics by Use of MAAC Assistance After Exit, Former Kansas City Area, 1996 Recipients, Survey Respondents Only

Characteristic	No Use	Less than 1 Service per Year	More than 1 Service per Year
Household income	$1,425	$1,150	$775
Respondent median monthly earnings	$980	$590	$372
Household median monthly earnings	$1,200	$868	$600
Work history			
Currently working	63%	53%	56%
Formerly worked	25%	41%	39%
Never worked	11%	6%	5%
No high school diploma or GED	20%	25%	31%
Presence of spouse/ partner	32%b	30%	13%
Food deprivation	22%b	37%	40%
N	128	49	84

Source: Mid America Assistance Coalition MAACLink database; Missouri Leavers' Survey.

We also examined receipt of both public[21] and private sources of assistance for this subgroup of leavers. If self-sufficiency is defined as neither public nor private support, only 16 percent of leavers would meet that criterion. Almost half (44 percent) received both private and public support, and one-third received only government support (see Table 9.14). Clearly, public support was more common than private aid.

Conclusion

Most former Missouri AFDC recipients continued to use some form of government and community-based supports more than two and a half years after leaving cash assistance. Thus, there is a continuing need for public sup-

Table 9.14. Use of Private and Public Support, 1997–2000, Kansas City Area Survey Respondents Only

	Percentage
Received both government and community support	44
Received government support only	33
Received neither government or community support	16
Received community support only	7
N	261

ports for low-income families. Although not all those who were eligible used support services at any one time, large majorities had used these services during the post-exit period. This implies that lack of knowledge of the program may not be the dominant or sole issue leading to low take-up rates in Missouri or in other states. The evidence from Kansas City shows that about half of former recipients used community-based emergency assistance after exiting AFDC. However, the frequency of assistance was low, and the amount of assistance was small for most recipients. From the evidence, it appears that leavers used community assistance for occasional emergencies and often as a supplement to government services.

Because of the sampling design, we were not able to discuss urban-rural differences reliably. However, it is worth noting that Kansas City area leavers were faring better than other leavers in terms of income and poverty status. Thus, it is not the case that the community assistance figures are based on leavers who are faring poorly relative to other leavers. Although this research presents data on only one cohort of welfare leavers, many of the results imply that they are generalizable to many who may leave the welfare rolls in the future. We were able to access data that noted the number of months of welfare receipt from 1992 to 1996. The average leaver had used AFDC for twenty-eight months during that period, a rather substantial length of time. This suggests that women who left AFDC in the fourth quarter of 1996 were not necessarily short-term users who were somehow different from other recipients. In addition, when we compare past use of AFDC among those who did and did not receive benefits, no significant differences were seen. That is, past length of time on welfare did not help explain differences in take-up rates for other support services. Finally, although not reported in this chapter, we have analyzed similar data for a cohort of 1997 TANF leavers. The data for these two cohorts are very comparable.

By combining survey data with information from state and local administrative data systems, we were able to provide a more complete profile of the use of low-income services than would have been obtained from either data source alone. While state administrative data systems contain accurate counts of the number of former cash recipients who continue to access government supports, the survey data provide valuable and detailed information on the characteristics of the service recipients. Linking these sources resulted in an enhanced information resource to support policy and program refinements.

Notes

1. This project was conducted under a contract from the Local Investment Commission with funds from the Missouri Department of Social Services and from a grant (98ASPE300A) provided to the state by the Office of the Assistant Secretary for Planning and Evaluation, U.S. Department of Health and Human Services.

2. Recipients were determined to have left the welfare rolls if they remained off assistance for two consecutive months. Child-only cases were excluded from the study.

3. Data were collected under subcontract with ORC Macro.

4. Approximately 6 percent of the survey respondents were found to have left Missouri.

5. The MAAC data cover the core urban counties: Jackson, Clay, and Platte Counties in Missouri and Wyandotte and Johnson Counties in Kansas.

6. MAAC's Web site, www.maaclink.org, provides more information on their organization and the services they provide.

7. All providers were asked to provide a value for each service given. For in-kind services, such as bags of food or clothing, guidelines were given to all agencies. That is, presumably the same bag of food would be assigned the same value regardless of the agency used. Those guidelines have remained constant over the study period.

8. Monthly income was ascertained for each person in a household aged sixteen and older from the following sources: earnings, child support, TANF, unemployment benefits, SSI, Survivor's Benefits or Veteran Payments, regular help from family or friends, Worker's Compensation, and all other sources. This was pretax income and did not include the EITC. Income data were collected for the month prior to interview. Since poverty thresholds are based on annual income, we annualized the monthly income to compare it with the thresholds.

9. For this report, we defined near poor to be under 185% of the poverty line. Extreme poverty is defined as 50 percent of the poverty line or less. For a household with three people, this would be approximately $6,923 in 1999.

10. The 50 percent figure was obtained by combining information from the survey and TANF records, since each source alone would underrepresent reality. When asked, survey respondents may have elected not to report returns, with the result that the administrative records would be more complete. On the other hand, leavers who returned to TANF in another state would be missed in the administrative files.

11. In Missouri, the income ceiling to receive CHIP is 300 percent of the poverty line.

12. The federal eligibility for Food Stamps stops at 130 percent of the poverty line. Using this as a guideline, we estimated whether households would be eligible based on the household income reported in the survey.

13. To receive a child care subsidy in Missouri, family income must be less than 130 percent of the poverty line. In addition, a parent must also demonstrate a need for child care due to employment, education, job training, or other specified need. Households were defined as eligible if they met the income criteria, contained an employed respondent, and had a child under age thirteen. This is a conservative estimate of eligible households, in that we were unable to model all of the activities that could qualify a mother for assistance. Similarly, our estimates of eligibility for child care are conservative, presenting eligibility only at the time of the interview rather than for the entire post exit period. For example, in some households, younger children could have aged out of the eligible category, and work status might also have changed over time.

14. The local housing authority manages public housing. Section 8 assistance refers to subsidies provided directly to owners, who then apply those subsidies to the rents charged to low-income tenants.

15. The survey did not ask about waiting lists for housing assistance, so we could not determine the number of households that desired such assistance but were unable to receive it.

16. In this section, "time of the survey" refers to either the day of the survey or the calendar month preceding it.

17. *Services* is defined as a benefit unit. If a person received both food and utility assistance at one visit to a community agency, this would be counted as two units of service.

18. All providers are asked to report a value for each service given. For in-kind services, such as bags of food or clothing, guidelines are given to all agencies. That is, presumably, the same bag of food would be assigned the same value, regardless of the agency providing the service. Those guidelines remained constant over the study period.

19. Many leavers had not been on AFDC for all three years prior to exit.

20. We determined some individual characteristics from the state administrative files, including age and number of children, as well as returns to TANF and Food Stamps. In addition, information is available on quarterly wages through unemployment insurance (UI) records. UI records do not cover all sectors of employment. The most notable exceptions were agricultural workers and federal employees.

21. Public support is defined as use of TANF, Medicaid, Food Stamps, child care subsidies, public housing, and WIC.

References

Dunton, N., Mosley, J., and Butcher, L. *Analysis of Non-Response*. Kansas City, Mo.: Midwest Research Institute, 2001.

Mosley, J., Dunton, N., and Butcher, L. *Socioeconomic Outcomes for Former Missouri AFDC Recipients: Report on 1996 Exit Cohort*. Kansas City, Mo.: Midwest Research Institute, 2001.

NANCY DUNTON *is the director of the Center for Health and Social Research at Midwest Research Institute, Kansas City, Missouri.*

JANE MOSLEY *is a senior researcher at the Center for Health and Social Research at Midwest Research Institute, Kansas City, Missouri.*

LOLA BUTCHER, *a graduate of the University of Missouri School of Journalism, wrote the questionnaire used to gather the data reported in this chapter.*

10
*This chapter examines ongoing efforts in Arizona to remove
barriers to self-sufficiency. It reports on three areas in which
difficulties in the implementation of existing policy were
identified and policy initiatives were developed to provide
more effective support to those leaving welfare.*

Managing the Transition to Self-Sufficiency: Changing State Policies to Provide Better Support to Clients Leaving Welfare

Karen Westra

Along with other states, Arizona has sought to implement welfare reforms that support the transition of welfare recipients to self-sufficient citizens. Given this goal, the dramatic caseload reduction that has occurred in Arizona is a positive development but one that must be followed up with an ongoing reexamination of barriers to self-sufficiency. Even more important, such ongoing reexaminations must be accompanied by a determination to use the resulting information to reform policy. This chapter addresses this ongoing effort in Arizona by reporting on three areas in which difficulties in the implementation of existing policy were identified and, through administrative discussions, policy initiatives were developed to provide more effective support to those leaving welfare.

Arizona Leaver Study

On September 14, 1998, the Arizona Department of Economic Security (ADES) was awarded a grant from the U.S. Department of Health and Human Services (DHHS) for research on the status of individuals and families who leave the Arizona Temporary Assistance for Needy Families (TANF) program. This comprehensive study examined the reasons clients left the state's welfare rolls in record numbers, what happened to them after they left, and how this phenomenon relates to the policy and provisional aspects of welfare reform. The study included a quantitative analysis of administrative data from unemployment insurance, cash assistance, Food Stamps, Medicaid, child care, child support, child protective services, and community services automated systems to determine wages, recidivism, and use of ADES benefits.

In addition, a random sample (1,140 leavers with 821 completed interviews) was selected for intensive interviews. The survey provided more in-depth information about reasons for exiting cash assistance use of other services and captured respondents' perceptions of their experiences and current status. The final report of the Arizona Cash Assistance Exit Study (Westra and Routley, 2000) documents both the positive and negative findings of the research. This chapter highlights and focuses exclusively on three barriers to self-sufficiency:

Case-closing policies (sanctions) were found to have a disproportionately negative effect on those most in need of policy supports in order to achieve self-sufficiency.

Many leavers who appear to be eligible for Food Stamps are not receiving them.

Many leavers who appear to be eligible for Medicaid coverage as a temporary support are nonetheless not receiving this benefit.

For each of these three areas, we describe the nature of the problem and then discuss the policy responses that have been developed to address the problem.

Administrative Information Needs

In Arizona, as in many other states, the goal of welfare reform was to promote client self-sufficiency. The TANF program allowed states to experiment with new and innovative policies in an effort to reach the goal. However, because the policies were untested, there was also concern that the experiment might backfire, and children and their families would suffer.

The Arizona welfare leaver study was particularly relevant because it was an outgrowth of a demand for answers. The demand came from advocacy groups, legislators, and policymakers within the ADES who wanted to know whether we were helping or hurting our constituents. For example, there were particular concerns about a displacement of services. Might we simply be trading cash assistance for food banks and homeless shelters? Other concerns were about the fairness of the policies: Were the policies being applied equally to different groups and in different parts of the state? And, finally, there was a nationwide concern that the reduction in the welfare rolls meant additional hardships for many who now had neither adequate employment nor sufficient public support. The Arizona study sought to address these concerns and in a way that was credible to all. The ADES made a public commitment to advocacy groups and to members of the Arizona legislature that it would conduct a rigorous study that would be comprehensive and relevant to public policy.

Identified Problems and Policy Responses

The Arizona study allayed some fears. For example, the study found no increase in the number of substantiated child protective services reports or out-of-home placements following exit from cash assistance. Individuals who left cash assistance were found to be less reliant on additional supports such as free or discounted meals for their children or assistance from food banks. They were also less likely to be without food and were less likely to be forced to move or have their utilities shut off because they were unable to pay their bills (Westra and Routley, 2000). The study did, however, identify several areas of concern. The three issues addressed in this section represent areas in which the data supported considering alternatives for policy reform.

Case-Closing Policies (Sanctions). Based on prior state policies (the EMPOWER initiative) and elements of the Personal Responsibility and Work Opportunity Reconciliation Act (PRWORA) of 1996, welfare recipients were subject to an automatic progressive sanctioning for noncompliance with the Arizona Jobs program, child support enforcement, school attendance, and immunization. Failure to meet program requirements on the part of the client results in a reduction of the cash assistance grant amount by 25 percent in the month following noncompliance. Clients who remain in noncompliance have their cash assistance reduced to 50 percent of the original grant amount in the second month. If the program requirements still are not met by the third month, the cash assistance case is closed. The case must then remain closed for one month before clients can comply with program rules and reinstate their benefit.

Administrative data gathered for the study indicated that 20 percent of the cases were closed due to a sanction. Individuals from these cases are different, both demographically and experientially, from their nonsanctioned counterparts. Specifically, the adults in the sanctioned cases

- Are less likely to have completed high school (45 percent versus 54 percent)
- Have less income from reported quarterly wages ($1,090–$2,216 versus $1,359–$2,717)
- Are more likely to report that in their opinion, they are worse off now than when they were on cash assistance (23 percent versus 13 percent)
- Are more likely to be of African American (13 percent versus 9 percent) or Hispanic origin (39 percent versus 33 percent), and less likely to be Native American (8 percent versus 15 percent) or Caucasian (39 percent versus 42 percent)
- Are more likely to live in urban Maricopa County (62 percent versus 49 percent)

Administrative Discussions. The ADES was concerned that sanctions were falling more heavily on those already facing challenges such as lower education and lower wages. Further, the ADES also was concerned that African Americans and Hispanics were disproportionately represented among the sanctioned. These concerns suggested that while the goal of the sanctioning policy was to encourage individuals to work actively toward self-sufficiency, the ADES was not doing enough to reduce barriers that might prevent or hinder people from participating fully in the case management process. The ADES thus decided to take some bold moves to reach out to those who were at risk of being sanctioned in the hope that sanctioning would be avoided.

Policy Response. On August 1, 1999, the ADES implemented a program targeted to families with multiple barriers to employment. The Employment Transition Program (ETP) provides direct support and intervention services to TANF families, including those who have received sanctions. The ADES contracts with ETP providers for services that include family assessments, housing search and relocation, intensive family preservation services, supportive intervention and guidance, counseling, mental health and substance abuse counseling, case management, child care, parenting skills training, transportation, emergency services, parent aide services, shelter services with parental consent, and respite services.

Among its other goals, this program is intended to ensure that sanction decisions are made only after additional review. For example, if a good-cause reason for an individual's lack of compliance with the Jobs program cannot be found, the staff refers the participant to the ETP. That referral is made prior to an initial sanction. Additional referrals are made if the individual receives a first sanction or complies with program provisions but later is out of compliance once again.

The ETP provider or the client must contact the ADES within thirty days of the referral. If the individual agrees to participate in the services, the sanction will not be imposed. ETP providers are required to try to contact individuals to give them maximum opportunity to take advantage of the services offered. This includes letters, telephone calls, and home visits by the providers. A sanction will be imposed only if the individual refuses or terminates ETP services or if the individual cannot be reached after multiple attempts. In order to take extra care that the ADES has done its part to try to reduce barriers to compliance with the Jobs program, effective July 17, 2000, a Jobs supervisor must approve all sanctioning actions before they can be implemented. This includes a review of the good-cause determination, as well as attempts to refer the participant to the ETP.

Reduction in Food Stamp Use. ADES expected a reduction in cash assistance participation under welfare reform. A similar decline in participation in the Food Stamp program was not anticipated. Based on earnings reported in the unemployment insurance database, most leavers appear eligible for Food Stamps. Forty-eight percent of the cases in Arizona's cash assistance exit study reported no earnings in the quarter following case closure. Those who had earnings reported an average of $2,142 during the quarter. In spite of these low earnings, only 50 percent of leavers received Food Stamps in the quarter following case closure. Approximately one year following exit from cash assistance, 44 percent of the surveyed individuals reported that they were receiving Food Stamps.

Administrative Discussions. ADES believes that everyone who is eligible for and needs Food Stamps should receive this assistance. There was concern, therefore, that leavers were not properly informed by caseworkers that they might be eligible for this form of assistance, that the message was not understood, or that leavers were not availing themselves of the services even when they were aware of the availability. This concern was borne out in the survey finding that only about 50 percent of the survey respondents recalled being notified by ADES that they may continue to receive Food Stamps. Although ADES communicated the information through letters and personal contact, roughly half of respondents had either not received or not understood the necessary information. Of those who were not receiving Food Stamps, 58 percent believed they were ineligible. This finding that many who likely were eligible for Food Stamps believed themselves to be ineligible was taken by ADES administrators as evidence of a need for greater outreach to this population.

Policy Response. ADES took several steps to ensure that those eligible for Food Stamps were informed of their eligibility and to make it easier for leavers to receive the services needed. First, ADES extended office hours for determining program eligibility beyond the normal 8 A.M. to 5 P.M business hours. Depending on staffing, staff also may work during extended hours. Eligibility offices open as early as 7:00 A.M. and close as late as 7:00 P.M. Some offices have Saturday hours as well. Clients may also schedule an appointment outside of the business schedule if necessary.

As a second step, the ADES is implementing an innovative food bank outreach project. This project is TANF-funded and involves placing Jobs participants as volunteers and TANF eligibility interviewers into selected food banks. These staff work together to assist clients in applying for benefits and completing on-the-spot interviews when possible. This service also provides participants with the job skills they need to find work. These specialized workers refer applicants to the local TANF office, where they are interviewed by designated staff on the same day they arrive. The funding subsidizes the equipment needed to carry out the project, including PCs, printers, electronic benefit transfer equipment, FAX machines, and telephone lines. The project is being implemented in four locations within metropolitan Phoenix.

Reduction in Medical Assistance Use. Similar to the problem with Food Stamps, only 58 percent of the adults in the study continued to receive Medicaid benefits in the quarter following exit from cash assistance. When asked about health care coverage, survey respondents indicated that

- They are more likely to lack needed medical attention when not receiving cash assistance.
- Twenty-three percent of them had one or more children in their home with a chronic health condition.
- Forty percent of the adults and 26 percent of the children had no health insurance a little more than one year following exit through Medicaid, an employer, or any other source. Of those who were not receiving publicly funded medical assistance, 66 percent said they did not believe they were eligible, and 56 percent said they did not believe their children were eligible.

Administrative Discussions. As with Food Stamps, the concern was that agency policy was not being implemented to ensure that those eligible for services were informed of their potential eligibility, that the method of communication was effective, and that it was convenient for eligible leavers to access the services. Not only did this underenrollment represent additional hardships for those with health care needs, it also was a likely source of TANF recidivism, wherein some who had left welfare later returned to the TANF rolls because of a lack of non-Medicaid health insurance. ADES administrators recognized the need to streamline the eligibility process and make it less of a barrier to services.

Policy Response. ADES has taken steps to make it easier for individuals to continue to receive Medicaid. In addition to making appointments available beyond typical business hours, the face-to-face interview requirement for redetermination of Medicaid benefits was waived in May 1999. Certification periods for medical eligibility were extended from six to twelve months. Application forms are mailed to families when they are scheduled to have their eligibility redetermined.

In addition, the Jobs program has designated staff to perform outreach and provide educational activities and material to ensure that TANF participants are aware of Medicaid benefits available to them and their children, both while receiving cash assistance and when they become ineligible for cash assistance. In addition, these staff promote other programs related to job retention such as Transitional Child Care, Jobs Program Transition Services, the Arizona Partners Mentoring Program, Employment Incentives, Volunteer Income Tax preparation, and other community-based assistance programs.

Although not a direct result of the Arizona study, it is worth noting that health care coverage is being expanded by Proposition 204. One of the most important provisions of Proposition 204 is the expansion of Medicaid eligibility up to 100 percent of the Federal Poverty Level (FPL). Prior to Proposition 204, parents were eligible who were at 36 percent of the FPL, and medically indigent and medically needy men, women, and couples were eligible if they were at or below 38 percent of the federal poverty level. It is estimated that this change in eligibility will cover an additional 110,000 to 130,000 adults.

In sum, ADES is beginning to address the challenge of how to streamline the process. The challenge is how to seek out those who need the health insurance and get them enrolled. As first steps, ADES will be providing outreach to parents of young children who are currently enrolled, as well as those who are receiving Food Stamps but are not enrolled in Arizona's expanded Medicaid program. ADES will be sending letters to both of these groups of individuals suggesting that they apply.

Conclusion

The Arizona Cash Assistance Exit Study (Westra and Routley, 2000) uncovered some areas of concern regarding the application of sanctions and the use of Food Stamps and medical insurance. These findings have been used as an opportunity to examine existing policies and provide new supports to individuals in their ongoing efforts to become or remain self-sufficient. The examples of how the study findings have led to policy responses are important in that they connect the results presented in this volume with administrative actions. The examples are important also because they provide an opportunity to reflect on ways that the Arizona study was useful in guiding policy reform.

There are several conclusions from this reflection that have relevance for other policy studies. First, the study was of particular relevance in that it was not merely an academic exercise developed by ADES researchers. Instead, it was borne out of questions being asked by advocacy groups, legislators, and ADES policymakers. These constituents had a genuine interest in knowing the impact of significant changes in the services being offered to a vulnerable population. Second, the results of the study were presented in a timely fashion while the issues were still relevant. And, finally, the scrutiny the study received from all of these constituents ensured that the study was rigorous and thorough and that the findings would result in policy changes.

Reference

Westra, K. L., and Routley, J. *Cash Assistance Exit Study: First Quarter 1998 Cohort* (Final Report). Arizona Department of Economic Security, 2000.

KAREN WESTRA *is acting systems and automation administrator in the Division of Child Support Enforcement, Systems and Automation Administration, Arizona Department of Economic Security.*

11

This chapter summarizes the findings from the studies presented in this volume, examines the broader lessons for research on leavers, and identifies next steps for policymakers and researchers.

Conclusions: Implications for Policy Reform and Policy Research

E. Michael Foster, George Julnes

This volume has focused on developing our understanding of welfare reform. Beginning with a review of the enduring questions surrounding social welfare policies and an overview of a federally funded series of welfare leavers studies, it then offers more detailed analyses of the experiences of leavers in three states: Georgia, Illinois, and Missouri. Those studies combine both administrative and survey data and draw on a variety of analytical methods. The results of these more detailed analyses are generally consistent with the national trends identified by Isaacs (Chapter Three) and by McClintock and Lowe (Chapter Two) but provide additional insights into how leavers are faring and some insights into the reasons. These studies also reveal the strengths and weaknesses of research of this type. In this concluding chapter, we summarize the findings from the studies presented here, highlight the broader lessons for research on leavers, and identify next steps for policymakers and researchers.

Common Findings

In Chapter Three, Isaacs wisely cautions readers about linking between-state differences in study results to cross-state variation in policies. The former may reflect methodological differences in the studies, and we see substantial variation even among the studies included here. Different authors, for example, define the population of interest differently. In order to understand post-exit access to Medicaid and Food Stamps, Anderson, Halter, and Schuldt (Chapter Eight) exclude cases that have returned to the TANF rolls, while other studies include those cases. The Georgia studies (Chapters Five and Six) highlight the role of child-only cases, which are excluded from the other studies.

Although between-study differences may indeed be difficult to interpret, there is a compelling similarity of findings among the studies included here and between these findings and those reviewed by Isaacs. First, the studies generally indicate that the leavers have joined the ranks of the working poor. In Georgia, Illinois, and Missouri, the majority of leavers were working at the time of the survey, and administrative data reveal that the vast majority of leavers worked at some point in the years following exit (Chapters Five and Nine). Even when employed, however, many leavers and their families still live in poverty and rely on various forms of government support.

A second common finding, therefore, is that leavers generally are not self-sufficient. This raises the issues of the proper goal of welfare reform and what constitutes a successful exit. Julnes, Hayashi, and Anderson (Chapter Seven) reported that based on self-reported experiences, only one in five leavers were unequivocal post-exit successes. A distinguishing feature of these most successful leavers is that they have the types of jobs that include health care benefits. As Isaacs notes, families were generally not self-sufficient under the old system. However, these findings highlight the fact that welfare reform has moved families only part of the way from dependency to self-sufficiency. These findings also call into question the notion that the old system was the underlying cause of dependency: eliminating AFDC has not caused dependency (broadly defined) to vanish.

Although complete self-sufficiency may be the exception, a third common finding is that despite high poverty rates, many leavers do not use services and programs for which they apparently are eligible. The studies in this volume are generally consistent with research nationwide: Medicaid enrollment is lower for adults than for children but exceeds participation in Food Stamps, with both falling below rates one would anticipate (Chapters Six, Eight, and Nine). To some extent, these patterns are easily explained. Expansions of Medicaid enrollment have opened opportunities for children to retain coverage; adults, on the other hand, generally must rely on transitional assistance that lasts for no more than one year. Nonetheless, a substantial fraction of children who are apparently eligible for Medicaid are not enrolled. Fairly low rates of Food Stamp use are puzzling as well, especially in the light of fairly high levels of reported food inadequacy found among Georgia leavers (Chapter Five).

Expanding on this question of use of services, both Dunton, Mosley, and Butcher (Chapter Nine) and Anderson, Halter, and Schuldt examine combinations of the use (and nonuse) of Food Stamps, Medicaid, child care subsidies, and other programs. The results from Missouri reveal the somewhat troubling finding that the failure to use available services extends across programs. For example, leavers who are receiving Food Stamps are 50 percent more likely to have a person in the household who is enrolled in

Medicaid. Anderson, Halter, and Schuldt's work reveals that although leavers typically use one or more support services at some point after exit, they rarely package services in a manner that would best support post-TANF work efforts. Anderson, Halter, and Schuldt explore the reasons that leavers do not use services for which they are eligible. They report that a substantial minority of leavers have not applied for benefits because they mistakenly believe they are ineligible or because of system constraints, such as application hassles.

A final common finding is that all of the studies identify substantial heterogeneity among leavers. One source of this variation is geographical. Anderson, Halter, and Schuldt, for example, find that combined Medicaid and Food Stamps use in the Chicago area is less than half that in other parts of the state. Examining other sources of variation, Rickman, Bross, and Foster (Chapter Five) find that stability of employment plays a critical role in determining which leavers fare best. Past program status also explains some variability. Echoing a theme that Isaacs develops, Anderson, Halter, and Schuldt find that individuals whose cases are closed for noncooperation are less likely to receive Food Stamps or be enrolled in Medicaid after exit. Julnes, Hayashi, and Anderson find heterogeneity in leavers' needs for services such as child care and health insurance and that these differing needs explain much of the variation in post-exit well-being. Finally, Rickman and Foster (Chapter Six) identify substantial differences between child-only and single-parent cases.

Broader Lessons

These results—both the shared findings and the differences among the studies—highlight broader lessons for research on welfare leavers. The first involves the benefits of combining administrative and survey data. Administrative data offer several advantages. They allow one to examine large samples and include multiple cohorts of leavers. Second, these data allow for tracking families over time. These findings make it clear that the transition off welfare is only one of a series of a transitions that occur over time and, in many cases, is part of a lifetime of instability for the women involved. As Rickman, Bross, and Foster reveal, whether a leaver is working at a point in time offers only a limited snapshot of employment and its link to a successful transition off welfare. Furthermore, administrative data can offer an invaluable insight into what life was like for these families prior to welfare reform. Dunton, Mosley, and Butcher offer key data on the pre-exit use of community services. Several of the studies are able to examine time on welfare prior to reform as a key predictor of post-exit success. An added advantage of administrative data (not highlighted here) is that they may provide a more reliable measure of program involvement. It is not clear that self-reports provide a reliable picture of program participation, and especially of changes in participation over time.

Administrative data, however, suffer from several weaknesses that are apparent here. These data lack key information, such as the reasons families do not participate in programs. As the findings by Anderson, Halter, and Schuldt illustrate, survey information can offer important insights into the mechanisms underlying patterns of participation (and nonparticipation). As the survey data on household income make clear, unemployment insurance wage records offer an incomplete picture of a family's resources; these data fail to capture certain kinds of employment or the wages of other family members.

A second problem with administrative data involves coverage of individuals. As the results indicate, the group of individuals of greatest concern are those isolated individuals who are not succeeding and yet are involved in no programs. The state appears to have lost contact with these individuals entirely, and so the state's records are of little use. A third problem with administrative data (not highlighted here) involves a range of technical problems (for example, linking data from various sources or agencies). Thus, the first lesson from these studies is that both survey and administrative data are essential for understanding life after welfare.

These studies offer a second lesson—the value of multiplism—that follows from the limitations of post-exit data. In general, the studies were challenged in trying to represent what life would have been like for leavers had the pre-TANF system continued. As Isaacs notes, the studies try to approximate the necessary data in a variety of ways. Some of the studies are able to draw on administrative data for the pre-TANF period, but the range of information provided is limited. Another option for this pre-post approach is to ask respondents to comment on what their life was like prior to reform. Such reports suffer from a variety of problems, including unreliable recall. Even if respondents recalled prior events (and their timing) accurately, it is not clear what such pre- and postcomparisons really reveal given the steady economic growth and other policy changes (such as the Children's Health Insurance Program) implemented since 1996. Another possibility is to compare leavers and stayers, a strategy that Rickman and Foster pursued. Although such comparisons offer one estimate of how leavers would have fared had they stayed on the rolls, between-group differences are difficult to interpret. They potentially confound the effect of leaving welfare with factors driving differences in welfare use. These problems, then, highlight one of the contributions of multiplism in policy evaluation: the kinds of data needed for firm conclusions are almost never available, and yet decisions must be made. Multiplism, in this case combining the type of comparison that Rickman and Foster make with the relationships shown by Julnes, Fan, and Hayashi's structural equation modeling approach (Chapter Four), can help support those decisions.

A final lesson concerns the need to understand research on leavers within the surrounding sociocultural context. For example, it seems clear that understanding how leavers are faring requires that this research be embedded in the broader context of poor families. Assessing the degree of post-exit success that leavers experience has to include an understanding of the experiences of other working-poor families and of others who remain on TANF cash assistance. The definition of success also must be placed in the context of the multiple goals of welfare reform—increased employment effort, decreased recidivism, enhanced well-being, change in the culture of dependency—and the relative priority given to these goals. These priorities vary across stakeholder groups and vary with fluctuations in the health of the national economy.

What Is Next for Policymakers and Researchers?

The research presented here highlights several next steps for policymakers and researchers and for collaboration and exchange involving the two groups. The first step is for states to undertake the sort of monitoring presented here as a routine part of running programs for the poor. Although the findings offer key insights into how programs affect poor families, the survey data are limited to groups of leavers who left TANF in a relatively short time window in the early stages of the reform effort. (The Georgia study is conducting a second wave of data collection that is not reported here.) As the administrative data make clear, however, a longitudinal perspective is invaluable, particularly because the fate of welfare leavers is influenced by so many factors, such as the strength of the economy and the changing characteristics of those leaving the rolls.

A second next step involves researchers. Continued effort is needed in refining the methodology used to conduct these studies. The need for such improvements is most apparent in the area of nonresponse. Response rates for the studies reported here are respectable relative to other leavers studies but are, in absolute terms, too low. When one-third or more of possible respondents do not participate in a survey, enormous uncertainty exists about the size and composition of that group of leavers who are facing the greatest challenges to moving off welfare successfully. Reason for optimism exists, however. Methodology for handling missing data is an area of active research in statistics (see, for example, the recent research on multiple imputation: Schafer, 1997; Schafer, 1999; Schafer and Olsen, 1998). Furthermore, the combination of administrative and survey data offers exciting possibilities for assessing and adjusting for missing data. In particular, unlike most survey efforts, welfare researchers often have extensive information on the individuals they are unable to interview. The studies presented here do compare survey respondents and nonrespondents using administrative data, but those comparisons are yet to be fully exploited.

A third area for future research involves both policymakers and researchers. Missing from this research is a key agent in the process of leaving welfare: the case worker and personnel in the local welfare office. In describing regional variation, Anderson, Halter, and Schuldt make some mention of the importance of these factors. However, none of the studies here includes characteristics of the case worker or of the policies of the county office in which he or she works. These factors seem essential to understanding how leavers fare, especially their involvement in programs designed to ease their movement off the rolls. This sort of research would require an extension of multiplism; the authors in this volume do not include researchers with an interest in organizations or public management. These researchers are essential to extending the studies along these lines.

Finally, a fourth area for future research involves a more refined focus on individuals who are struggling. At this point, it seems clear that policymakers and researchers have a fairly good understanding of how the average leaver is faring. Like the working poor in general, the lives of these individuals could be improved substantially by extending Medicaid coverage to more families (including adults) and improving program outreach. Similarly, making families aware of their eligibility for Food Stamps and the unearned income tax credit and reducing the burden of applying for these benefits would help as well. The group of leavers who are experiencing the greatest post-exit difficulties—those who are unplugged from both public and community-based support—have needs that are not as well understood. Lacking the social support as well as the psychological well-being needed to make a successful transition off welfare, this group likely will require more intensive or innovative program initiatives. This then raises the question of whether the final judgment on welfare reform, and efforts to modify it, should rest on our ability to link these most at-risk families and their children with the services and resources they need to achieve self-sufficiency and some minimal quality of life.

References

Schafer, J. L. *Analysis of Incomplete Multivariate Data.* New York: Chapman and Hall, 1997.
Schafer, J. L. "Multiple Imputation: A Primer." *Statistical Methods in Medical Research,* 1999, 8, 3–15.
Schafer, J. L., and Olsen, M. K. "Multiple Imputation for Multivariate Missing-Data Problems." *Multivariate Behavioral Research,* 1998, 33, 545–571.

E. MICHAEL FOSTER *is associate professor of health policy and administration at The Pennsylvania State University.*

GEORGE JULNES *is assistant professor of psychology with the Research and Evaluation Methodology Program and director of the Center for Policy and Program Evaluation at Utah State University.*

INDEX

---

*ASPE, Assistant Secretary for Planning and Evaluation

Back Issue/Subscription Order Form

Copy or detach and send to:
Jossey-Bass, 989 Market Street, San Francisco CA 94103-1741

Call or fax toll free!
Phone 888-378-2537 6AM-5PM PST; Fax 800-605-2665

Back issues: Please send me the following issues at $27 each.
(Important: please include series initials and issue number, such as EV77.)

1. EV _____

_____

_____

$ _____ Total for single issues

$ _____ Shipping charges (for single issues *only;* subscriptions are exempt from shipping charges): Up to $30, add $5^{50} • $30^{01}–$50, add $6^{50} $50^{01}–$75, add $7^{50} • $75^{01}–$100, add $9 • $100^{01}–$150, add $10 Over $150, call for shipping charge.

Subscriptions   Please ❏ start   ❏ renew my subscription to *New Directions for Evaluation* for the year ___ at the following rate:

❏ Individual: $69 U.S./Canada/Mexico; $93 International

❏ Institutional: $145 U.S.; $185 Canada; $219 International
NOTE: Subscriptions are quarterly, and are for the calendar year only. Subscriptions begin with the spring issue of the year indicated above. For shipping outside the U.S., please add $25. Prices are subject to change.

$ _____ Total single issues and subscriptions (CA, IN, NJ, NY and DC residents, add sales tax for single issues. NY and DC residents must include shipping charges when calculating sales tax. NY and Canadian residents only, add sales tax for subscriptions.)

❏ Payment enclosed (U.S. check or money order only.)

❏ VISA, MC, AmEx, Discover Card #_____ Exp. date_____

Signature _____ Day phone _____

❏ Bill me (U.S. institutional orders only. Purchase order required.)

Purchase order #_____

Name _____

Address _____

_____

Phone_____ E-mail _____

For more information about Jossey-Bass Publishers, visit our Web site at:
www.josseybass.com   **PRIORITY CODE = ND1**

CONTENTS

OTHER TITLES AVAILABLE IN THE
NEW DIRECTIONS FOR EVALUATION SERIES
Jennifer C. Greene, Gary T. Henry, Editors-in-Chief

Coordinating Multiple Perspectives of Welfare Outcomes

Recent headlines have highlighted the dramatic decrease in TANF caseloads experienced nationwide ("Off Welfare, Not Faring So Well," 2000). Although these figures suggest that TANF is a success, numerous researchers have challenged this conclusion as simplistic. They argue, for example, that caseloads were declining even before PRWORA (Ellwood, 2000). They add that caseload size is a narrow indicator of program success that provides little indication of the self-sufficiency of former TANF recipients (Young, 2000).

Such debates are common in the policy arena, but it is useful to highlight one source of controversy in the current welfare debate. Much of the available information involves simple descriptive data drawn from administrative files. Although reliance in policymaking on what amounts to monitoring data has been criticized, as seen in literature on the performance measurement movement (Perrin, 1998), efforts to improve government policies increasingly rely on such data. This reliance reflects the general problem that data appropriately collected for one purpose often are employed unreflectively in service of another purpose. To improve our use of available data and guide our collection of additional data, it is important to be clear about the multiple purposes that evaluation is called on to address and the multiple methods that are available for pursuing particular sets of purposes (Mark, Henry, and Julnes, 2000). This implies a strategic approach to coordinating multiple perspectives in evaluation.

Making Use of Multiple Perspectives

The idea that evaluators are more effective when using multiple perspectives is not new. Cook and his colleagues (Cook, 1985; Shadish, Cook, and Houts, 1986) proposed critical multiplism as a nonfoundational approach that uses multiple perspectives to compensate for the limitations of any single perspective or method. According to Cook, this multiplism could involve multiple, program theories, operationalization of constructs, methodology paradigms, professional affiliations of investigators, and contexts for inquiry.

The basic insights of critical multiplism continue to be developed in evaluation. For example, Caracelli and Greene (1997) argue for a mixed-method approach involving the coordination of different paradigms (such as the quantitative and qualitative paradigms). Nonetheless, despite such calls for multiplism, most evaluations and policy analyses are motivated and shaped by a single tradition. In part, this narrow focus often reflects the inertia that comes from training in a particular approach to evaluation. Another obstacle is that the complexity implied by critical multiplism can be immobilizing. Without some sense of priorities, arguments for multiple methods often devolve into recommendations to "do everything." Few, if any, evaluations can or should aspire to such comprehensiveness.